WHAT YOUR
ARE SAYING . . .

"*Social Emotional Well-Being for Educators* is a valuable resource. Michelle Trujillo has created a Framework for Social Emotional Well-Being that is aligned with the five SEL competencies as defined by CASEL and which provides practical ideas, strategies, and opportunities for educators to nourish their own well-being and ultimately that of young people."

—Karen Van Ausdal
Senior Director of Practice
The Collaborative for Academic, Social, and Emotional Learning (CASEL)

"She had me at 'Throwing Out the Lesson Plan.' Michelle Trujillo's latest book offers some of the most relevant advice I've heard in the wake of pandemic education—starting with throwing out the lesson plan! These are not normal times, and we should not be conducting business as usual in our schools. In fact, even under the best of circumstances, some of our most impactful teaching moments happen when we are willing to be present in the moment and connect with our students on a deeper level. This book will help us do exactly that, and, equally important, learn to care for our own well-being along the way."

—Amy Cranston
Executive Director
SEL4CA: Social Emotional Learning Alliance for California

"As a life-long educator, Michelle Trujillo understands that SEL skills are the essence of who we are as human beings. She knows through her work in alternative education that SEL skills can serve as our North Star when our life's journey presents rough seas. *Social Emotional Well-Being for Educators* empowers us with reflection opportunities, practical strategies, and a framework for being that will light our way as we encounter the challenges found in uncharted waters."

—Maurice J. Elias
Director
Rutgers Social-Emotional and Character Development Lab

"*Social Emotional Well-Being for Educators* is a necessary read for anyone working within a school community. An educator's well-being is vital to supporting the whole child, mitigating instructional loss, and integrating social emotional learning into the culture of the school community. Michelle's newest book provides a framework for adult SEL that is authentic, practical, and empowering!"

—Douglas Fisher
Professor of Educational Leadership, San Diego State University
Teacher Leader, Health Sciences High

"If you want to know more about enhancing your social emotional well-being while making a tremendous impact on students, then this is the book for you. It is a delightful guide full of important information, especially when there is nothing left in your emotional tank. Michelle Trujillo takes readers on a wonderful journey into the work of social emotional learning and helps us continue to be empathetic, kind, and understanding educators. There is no other book like it!

—Pam Gilmartin
Elementary School Principal
Carson City, NV

"Michelle Trujillo has a voice that speaks directly to each reader and provides a deeper connection to the applicable content she provides in this book. It's obvious from her writing and storytelling that the well-being of others is one of her core values. *Social Emotional Well-Being for Educators* will have an immediate and positive impact on students and teachers alike."

—Keeley Keller
Director of Professional Programs
Learners Edge

"*Social Emotional Well-Being for Educators* is more than a book about adult SEL or adult self-care—it is about a way of being for teachers which will affect their relationships with students and their ability to better handle the challenges of teaching in 2022 and beyond. This important book is grounded in good science and provides well-scaffolded tools that can help teachers be more self-aware and reflective about their behaviors. It is also grounded in good practice and will help teachers to be more empathic and to intentionally act in a way that supports equity and their connectedness with students and others."

—David Osher
Vice President and Fellow
American Institutes for Research (AIR)

"Teachers, school counselors, and other school staff will find this book a welcome support to deal with the stress and strains during COVID times and beyond. There are two strategies for handling these tough times—tolerating them or pausing just long enough to grow from them. This hands-on book offers the strategies needed to pause and grow."

—Sara Rimm-Kaufman
Author, *SEL from the Start: Building Skills in K-5*
Professor of Education, University of Virginia

"Michelle Trujillo has created a framework that integrates the concepts of adult SEL and equity in a way that is applicable and meaningful. She ties the core components of social emotional learning with specific competencies for adults in a 'way of being' for educators. Stakeholders need materials like this book to help guide them through the process by focusing on relevance, recognition, reflection, and making it real. Michelle Trujillo describes these concepts in concrete detail that will help our educators work through roadblocks to their personal well-being. I highly recommend this book for all educators."

—Jennifer Rogers
LPC, Author, Counselor, Professional Learning Facilitator
Rogers Training Solutions, LLC

Social Emotional Well-Being for Educators

To

Corey and Dani

As you have grown into your adult selves,

your dad and I are constantly inspired by

your passion for life and appreciation of the journey!

This book is dedicated to both of you with all of our love.

Social Emotional Well-Being for Educators

Michelle L. Trujillo

FOR INFORMATION:

Corwin

A SAGE Company

2455 Teller Road

Thousand Oaks, California 91320

(800) 233-9936

www.corwin.com

SAGE Publications Ltd.

1 Oliver's Yard

55 City Road

London EC1Y 1SP

United Kingdom

SAGE Publications India Pvt. Ltd.

B 1/I 1 Mohan Cooperative Industrial Area

Mathura Road, New Delhi 110 044

India

SAGE Publications Asia-Pacific Pte. Ltd.

18 Cross Street #10-10/11/12

China Square Central

Singapore 048423

President: Mike Soules

Associate Vice President
and Editorial Director: Monica Eckman

Publisher: Jessica Allan

Associate Content
Development Editor: Mia Rodriguez

Editorial Intern: Ricardo Ramirez

Production Editor: Amy Schroller

Copy Editor: Amy Hanquist Harris

Typesetter: C&M Digitals (P) Ltd.

Proofreader: Talia Greenberg

Cover Designer: Janet Kiesel

Marketing Manager: Olivia Bartlett

Printed in the United States of America

Library of Congress Cataloging-in-Publication Data

Names: Trujillo, Michelle L., 1967- author.

Title: Social emotional well-being for educators / Michelle L. Trujillo.

Description: Thousand Oaks, California : Corwin, 2022. | Includes bibliographical references.

Identifiers: LCCN 2021045817 | ISBN 9781071866856 (paperback) | ISBN 9781071866863 (epub) | ISBN 9781071866870 (epub) | ISBN 9781071866887 (pdf)

Subjects: LCSH: Teachers—Mental health. | Educators—Mental health. | Self-care, Health. | Well-being.

Classification: LCC LB2840 .T784 2022 | DDC 371.102—dc23/eng/20211013

LC record available at https://lccn.loc.gov/2021045817

This book is printed on acid-free paper.

22 23 24 25 10 9 8 7 6 5 4 3 2 1

CONTENTS

For resources related to
Social Emotional Well-Being for Educators,
please visit the companion website at
resources.corwin.com/
SocialEmotionalWellBeingforEducators.

THROWING OUT
THE LESSON PLAN . . .

It is April 2020—springtime. A time that traditionally represents a unique juxtaposition for educators in that there is a feeling of being overwhelmed that always accompanies the assessment season and end-of-school-year preparations, and at the same time, an eager anticipation for summertime, which typically brings opportunities for educators to relax, renew, and rejuvenate. This year is different, however. A global pandemic, caused by COVID-19, is shaking normalcy to its core. It has forced school closures across our nation and has left students, families, and educators feeling confused, disappointed, frustrated, and isolated. Although I have found gifts in the challenges, like uninterrupted quality time with my family and more quiet time than I typically experience, I find that I am unsettled as I think about the world of education in which I am enthusiastically entrenched.

This morning, I fill my favorite mug with steaming coffee and walk to my standing desk in the home office I share with my husband. I retired several years ago from a fulfilling career as the principal at an alternative education high school. I have continued in my role as an educator—however, now as an author, speaker, and professional learning facilitator. I'm often on the road. But not today, nor over this past year and a half. Instead, today I am preparing to facilitate another virtual professional learning cohort from my home, with administrators who are participating from their homes. The administrators in my cohort are nearing the end of the school year, and they are in a quandary. How do they enjoy the summer and lean into the relaxation and renewal they've been craving, when they are preoccupied with how best to begin school in the fall? They wonder daily what tomorrow will bring. They have concerns and questions. How will they keep their staff and students safe? What will school look like now that the worst of the pandemic is behind us? How will they address the interrupted instruction, situational poverty, grief, loss, and other specific traumas that their students and a majority of their staff have experienced over the last year and a half? How do they best move forward when they don't know what they don't know? Most have relinquished the hope of feeling relaxed, refreshed, and renewed coming out of summer because anxiety, concern, and exhaustion dominate at the moment. So I prepare. I prepare to remind my administrative cohort and to remind myself, too, that, in the midst of all this uncertainty and adversity, there is something we do know. We are educators, and as educators, we are Ignitors of Hope!

(Continued)

(Continued)

At the same time, even Ignitors of Hope are human. We experience doubt, anticipate challenges, and yes, at times, lack hope ourselves. As this occurs to me, I realize that not only do educators need to be reminded of our role as Ignitors of Hope in the lives of our students, their families, and our colleagues, but we also need a means to sustain this role. And whatever this "means" is, it cannot be something that adds more to our already full plates. It cannot be something more we have to do, but a way in which we need to be. I began to reframe the idea of social emotional learning for adults as a quest for social emotional well-being—as in our state of being as adults and as educators. My thoughts move from my administrative cohort to their school staff members. All are people who work within the school system, striving to support students and families within the school community, and every one of them would benefit from nourishing their own social emotional well-being. This obvious epiphany caused for me a "throw-out-the-lesson-plan" moment! It's about a way of being!

I have always held this philosophy, but I realize my philosophy needs substance. Social emotional well-being must be our focus, and in it, we will find hope.

So I take a sip of my coffee and then a deep breath: It's time to get to work. I am eager to share with my administrative cohort the hope that can be found in focusing on our way of being!

Michelle L. Trujillo

That moment in my home office and the quality time with my administrative cohort later that day were the catalysts for my conviction to write this book. Let me provide some additional background. I have spent the last few years sharing the message that *we are Ignitors of Hope* with educators across the country. I began doing so because the reminder was needed. I noticed that the relaxed, refreshed, and renewed humans who stepped out of summer into the new school year typically didn't remain revitalized or restored. In fact, in my own experience as a former teacher and high school principal, within the first several weeks of every school year, I can remember that feeling of being overwhelmed begin to creep into my psyche and manifest itself in my body. Have you ever felt this way? If so, know that you are not alone.

In fact, in 2019 nearly three-quarters of teachers and 84 percent of school leaders described themselves as "stressed," and more than a third of education professionals experienced a mental health issue in the past academic year. Almost half (49 percent) believe their workplace is having a negative impact on their mental health and well-being.[1] One specific data point indicated that up to 43 percent of new teachers leave the profession within the first five years.[2]

Furthermore, according to the Centers for Disease Control (CDC), again in 2019, more than half of all US children have experienced some kind of trauma. Educators, regardless of their role in education, care deeply about students. And that means they are exposed to the traumas (e.g., secondary traumatic stress disorder) that students endure, such as poverty, addiction, mental health issues, neglect, abuse, racism, divorce, and grief. "Even if they have not endured trauma themselves, educators can begin exhibiting symptoms similar to those of their students—withdrawal, anxiety, depression, and chronic fatigue."[3]

Keep in mind, these statistics reflect educator feelings and experiences prepandemic! The trauma and hardships that our students, their families, our colleagues, and each of us have faced over this last year and a half create a reality that calls for *hope*! Additionally, the pandemic exposed the blatant inequities in the educational system based on access, race, and poverty. Likewise, a national racial reckoning catalyzed by the murder of George Floyd, also in 2020, implored educators to address societal racism and oppression because ultimately our implicit and explicit biases (and, yes, we all have them!) negatively impact our students, their families, our colleagues, and each of us as individuals and professionals. A future that is just, empathetic, and filled with compassion for humanity relies on hope in the form of action that leads to systemic change!

Here is another reality: As educators, we serve a phenomenal profession, an actual *vocation*, in which we have an opportunity to make a positive impact on the lives of young people, their families, and our colleagues every day! In fact, a positive school culture and academic achievement are anchored in a *way of being* that starts with each one of us as educators, regardless of whether school is located in a physical brick-and-mortar building, a virtual platform, or a combination of both. Yet with all of the responsibilities and concerns we carry in our personal lives, coupled with the normal demands of our vocation that are now amplified by new

---

[1] Donna Ferguson, "Record Levels of Stress 'Put Teachers at Breaking Point,'" *The Guardian*, Guardian News and Media, November 10, 2019, www.theguardian.com/education/2019/nov/10/stressed-teachers-at-breaking-point-says-report.

[2] David Perda, *Transitions Into and Out of Teaching: A Longitudinal Analysis of Early Career Teacher Turnover* (Philadelphia: University of Pennsylvania, 2013).

[3] Tim Walker, "'I Didn't Know It Had a Name': Secondary Traumatic Stress and Educators," *NEA Today*, December 18, 2019, neatoday.org/2019/10/18/secondary-traumatic-stress/.

expectations and requirements to keep ourselves and one another safe, it is only natural that we might feel overwhelmed, discouraged, or disheartened. We have all heard the saying, which is popularly attributed to Theodore Roosevelt, that *people will not care what we know until they know that we care.* In fact, as human beings serving our vocations with sincerity, we may very well experience these authentic feelings for the very reason that we *do* care.

So first and foremost, please know that you are appreciated. Let me say thank you for who you are as humans and for all you do as educators to serve your school communities! Let me also reiterate that, as educators, we are Ignitors of Hope. Our students and their families, our communities even, need us to serve in this role today more than ever before because as much as times are uncertain, people are uncertain too. Families want reassurance that their kids will be safe—that if and when they go to school, they will be taken care of—and they rely on us to provide that assurance. Yet educators need support too. We serve our vocations with passion, enthusiasm, and wisdom. Even in the midst of a global pandemic and social and racial turmoil, educators have responded with empathy, creativity, positivity, and flexibility, but that doesn't mean it's been easy. We often hear our supervisors tell us how important it is to take care of ourselves; we read educational articles about self-care and participate in workshops on adult social emotional learning (SEL). The reality is, however, that all of that just feels like more—more we have to do and more we have to give.

As an educator and advocate of hope, I know from experience that we do not need more to *do.* Equally important is that what we *do* is not as significant, to our lives and our relationships, as how we *be.* Don't laugh; I realize my grammar is off . . . however, intentionally so. Our state of being already *is.* Thus, hope will be found in a pursuit of how we *be.* It is not something more to add to our busy schedules; our thoughts, attitudes, and behaviors already exist. So doesn't it make sense to focus on our current state of being and ask ourselves if our thoughts, attitudes, words, and behaviors are working for us in a way that positively impacts our own well-being? The answer may lead us to understand that our current way of being may cause us to experience more stress. Or perhaps there is something about our current thoughts, attitudes, words, and behaviors that damage our relationships or jeopardize our physical, mental, or social health? We won't know unless we intentionally begin to attend to our social emotional well-being.

An epiphany of awareness, resolve, and growth can be found in focusing on social emotional learning for adults as a way of *being,* rather than a new skill we must learn, a task to complete, or a curriculum to implement. Likewise, cultivating our social emotional well-being will empower us, as humans and as educators, to nourish our mind, body, and spirit. Exploration of a Framework for

Social Emotional Well-Being through the journey that is this manuscript will ultimately lead to an opportunity for us to experience the feeling that we typically associate with summer. Let's call it a general experience of peace—peace within our heart, mind, body, spirit, and relationships. Furthermore, regardless of what time of year it is when you open the pages of this book, what is going on in the world, or where you are in your season of life, my hope and prayer is that when you reach the end you will not only *be* relaxed, refreshed, and renewed, but you will have ideas and strategies to sustain this way of being. Before we step into our journey, however, I'd like to give some context regarding my philosophy and perspective of social emotional learning.

ADULT SEL: JUST ANOTHER EDUCATIONAL INITIATIVE?

Life is filled with adversity, regardless of living through a pandemic. With any trial or tragedy, people tend to feel uncertain, helpless, overwhelmed, and even a bit afraid. All of these emotions, as well as others we might experience when confronting challenges, highlight the need for us to leverage our social emotional abilities in order to compassionately and effectively care for ourselves and, ultimately, others. We can and will ignite hope in in the lives of our students, colleagues, and ourselves when we first address our own *social emotional well-being.* Some call this adult SEL, which may cause you to wonder, "Is this just another passing educational initiative?" My answer is emphatically, "No, *and* it doesn't have to be called adult SEL!" Now, before I create pandemonium, let me take you back to my prior suggestion that "how we be" is more important than "what we do." I will specifically use the term "social emotional learning" and its common definition and competencies to give structure to *a way of being* that will ignite hope for our students, their families, our colleagues, and ourselves. It is the *way of being* that is embodied in this term that matters.

To take my disclaimer just one step further, I realize in the educational context the acronym SEL stands for **s**ocial **e**motional **l**earning, but couldn't it also stand for **s**kills for **e**nriched **l**iving, **s**tandards for **e**ducational **l**eadership, or even **s**ome **e**ssential **l**ifeskills? Okay, so maybe "lifeskills" isn't an actual word (actually, it is two: life skills), but do you get my point? The term "social emotional learning" may or may not weather the storm of change when the next educational initiative or program is introduced, but the need to promote skills that foster social emotional health and growth will always persevere. Let's consider the perspective of author, professor, and SEL expert Dr. Maurice Elias:[4]

> I think of SEL as the skills of *everydayship*. They are the set of skills that enable us to get along in the world. They are the foundation of all relationships and the engine of all actions. SEL skills are part of us from the moment we enter the earth and all the way through our journey through life. They are no more and no less important than oxygen. Adversity tests our skills and our character, which is part of my definition of SEL—that is, if SEL skills are the engine, or the propellers, then character and virtues are the rudder.

(Continued)

(Continued)

Dr. Maurice Elias

We require both for our journey. Rough seas, turbulent air, cratered roads, and other adversities challenge us, impede our progress, discourage us, sometimes throw us off course. We might try shortcuts and other expedient ways to cope with adversity, but those are the times to revisit our North Stars, our guiding virtues, and hold true to them. Easier said than done, but that is why SEL is so important—for adults and for children—during adversity.

These skills of *everydayship* to which Dr. Elias refers begin with us, as the adults within our school communities. How can we explicitly teach social emotional learning skills to our students or integrate SEL into our school culture if we do not understand, practice, or model the SEL skills that enhance our own social emotional health? The truth of the matter is that we can't, at least not in a way that is authentic. In order to ensure that adult SEL isn't just another educational initiative that passes with the tides of time, I suggest we reframe our thinking by emphasizing the term "social emotional well-being" when referring to adult SEL. As educators, if we focus on our own social emotional well-being as a *way of being*, it becomes meaningful, sustainable, and feasible to integrate into our daily personal and professional lives.

In order to effectively make this transition from adult SEL to social emotional well-being, it is essential to establish a connection to social emotional learning because this is the edifice that most educational entities are using to promote and support the well-being of students and staff alike. This connection begins with a review of the definition and structure that is most widely used and known within our educational system and provides us with a common language and a foundational understanding of the rationale for integrating social emotional learning into our school system in the first place.

By definition, according to the Collaborative of Academic, Social, and Emotional Learning (CASEL, 2020),[1]

> Social and emotional learning (SEL) is an integral part of education and human development. SEL is the process through which all young people and adults acquire and apply the knowledge, skills, and attitudes to develop healthy identities, manage emotions and achieve personal and collective goals, feel and show empathy for others, establish and maintain supportive relationships, and make responsible and caring decisions.

---

[1]"SEL Is . . ." *CASEL*, Nov. 2020, casel.org/what-is-sel/.

SEL advances educational equity and excellence through authentic school–family–community partnerships to establish learning environments and experiences that feature trusting and collaborative relationships, rigorous and meaningful curriculum and instruction, and ongoing evaluation. SEL can help address various forms of inequity and empower young people and adults to co-create thriving schools and contribute to safe, healthy, and just communities.

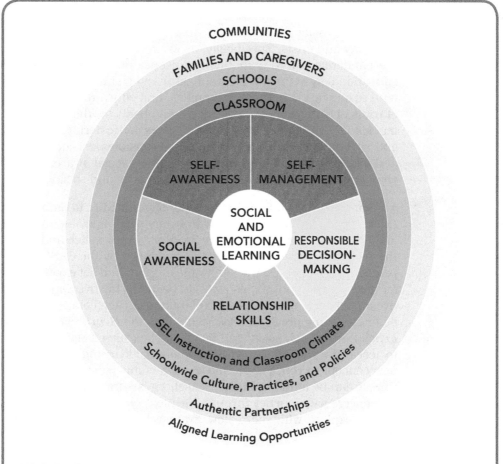

THE CASEL 5:

The CASEL 5 addresses five broad, interrelated areas of competence and examples for each: *self-awareness*, *self-management*, *social awareness*, *relationship skills*, and *responsible decision-making*. The CASEL 5 can be taught and applied at various developmental stages from childhood to adulthood and across diverse cultural contexts to articulate what students should know and be able to do for academic success, school and civic engagement, health and wellness, and fulfilling careers.

www.casel.org/what-is-SEL

As educators, we are aware that when we integrate social emotional learning into the culture of our schools or explicitly teach social emotional learning skills in our classrooms, there can be a positive impact on the entire school community. Research reveals improved student outcomes—academically and in regard to attitudes about self and others—reduced incidence of conduct problems, and decreased emotional distress[2] when we integrate social and emotional learning skills into our classrooms. Students involved in SEL programs with fidelity have demonstrated long-term impact, such as higher graduation rates and college attendance, better rates of employment and economic status, and decreased criminal record and substance abuse problems.[3] Furthermore, integration of SEL skills for students and *adults* is paramount in times of adversity and crisis. Specifically, as we have discussed previously, the pandemic placed a spotlight on issues of inequity within the educational system, and mental health and trauma-related issues tend to increase for students, families, and educators in the midst of trials or suffering of any kind. An emphasis on the five competencies of SEL can address these issues by fostering emotional and social connection, healthy and responsible decision-making, and a long overdue call to action to increase social awareness and change behavior in order to advocate for racial and social justice.

All that said, research on the benefits of adult SEL, to date, is not extensive. However, I can attest from my experience as a teacher and administrator that when we as educators practice and model the social emotional learning skills as defined by the CASEL competencies, not only are we better able to teach and set expectations for our students, but we also tend to be more effective and productive ourselves. A more explicit explanation of each competency can be found in my previous book, *Start With the Heart: Igniting Hope in Schools Through Social and Emotional Learning.* I encourage you to access it as a resource if social emotional learning is a relatively new concept to you. Furthermore, each competency as defined by CASEL can be found at https://casel.org/sel-framework/ for your reference. As we journey through the next section, however, I invite you to explore with me a new Framework for Social Emotional Well-Being.

---

[2]J. A. Durlak, R. P. Weissberg, A. B. Dymnicki, R. D. Taylor, and K. Schellinger, 2011, "The Impact of Enhancing Students' Social and Emotional Learning: A Meta-Analysis of School-Based Universal Interventions," *Raising Healthy Children* 82, no. 1: 402–32.

[3]J. D. Hawkins, R. Kosterman, R. F. Catalano, K. G. Hill and R. D. Abbott, 2005, "Positive Adult Functioning Through Social Development Intervention in Childhood: Long-Term Effects From the Seattle Social Development Project," *Archives of Pediatrics & Adolescent Medicine* 159, no. 1: 25–31; S., Aos, R., Lieb, J., Mayfield, M., Miller, and A., Pennucci, 2004. *Benefits and Costs of Prevention and Early Intervention Programs for Youth.* Olympia: Washington State Institute for Public Policy.

A FRAMEWORK FOR SOCIAL EMOTIONAL WELL-BEING

IT'S A WAY OF BEING!

Throughout this book, you have repeatedly read the term "way of being." I reference it so often because I have come to understand through experience that focusing on how we *be* as a philosophy and practice is the answer to combating initiative fatigue, vocational burnout, and personal stress. I want us to consider our *state of being* in the way in which we function as human beings in our daily walk in the world, both personally and professionally. With that consideration in mind, please take a moment to respond to the following prompts with the *first thought* that comes to mind:

When I awake in the morning, I typically feel:

_____

_____

When I am on my way to work (or preparing to step into my virtual day), I often think about:

_____

_____

When I walk in the door of my building (or log on to my computer to begin the day if still working virtually), the first thing I do is:

_____

_____

When I open my email inbox for the first time on a typical day, I feel:

_____

_____

When I begin interacting with others, my colleagues, or students, my demeanor tends to be:

_____

_____

(Continued)

(Continued)

During my lunch hour or break, I typically feel:

_____

_____

During my lunch hour or break, I typically notice:

_____

_____

I typically spend my lunch hour or break [doing what?]:

_____

_____

When I pass a student in the hallway, I typically:

_____

_____

When I pass a colleague in the hallway, I typically:

_____

_____

When I prepare to go home or shut down my computer for the day, I typically feel:

_____

_____

When I prepare to go home or shut down my computer for the day, I typically notice:

_____

_____

When I prepare to go home or shut down my computer for the day, I typically [do what?]:

_____

_____

When I arrive home (or engage back in my personal realm), I typically feel:

_____

_____

When I arrive home (or engage back in my personal realm), I typically think:

_____

_____

When I am with my family or friends, I typically feel:

_____

_____

When I have a moment to relax, I enjoy [doing what?]:

_____

_____

When I am in a situation that is unfamiliar, I typically feel:

_____

_____

When I am in a situation that is unfamiliar, I typically [do what?]:

_____

_____

(Continued)

(Continued)

When I observe injustice of any kind, I typically feel:

_____

_____

When I observe injustice of any kind, I typically [do what?]:

_____

_____

As you might guess, I could continue with additional prompts for pages. I will stop for now, however, to offer another task. Now, take time to review and ponder your first-thought responses. What do you notice? Is there anything that surprised you? Is there anything that you would like to change? If so, what would it take? Let your imagination run wild here . . . even if it doesn't seem feasible, what would it take to make a positive change in a specific area?

_____

_____

_____

_____

Thank you for taking time to share your first thoughts and to reflect on your answers. I asked you to do this because our emotions, feelings, and thoughts can often dictate our words, actions, or behaviors—in essence, our way of *being.* As people with full schedules, we don't often take time to reflect on what we feel, notice, think, and do. In fact, often we exist on autopilot, which can lead to the feeling of being overwhelmed and the burnout that is so common to educators. The Framework for Social Emotional Well-Being helps us to operationalize our wellness by presenting six specific *ways of being* that we can deliberately explore, cultivate, and apply in order to foster our social and emotional well-being. Let's take a look at the framework:

© 2021 Center for Learning and Well-Being

Social emotional well-being, by my subjective definition, is a *way of being* in which human beings feel, believe, and act in a way with each other (and themselves) that honors diversity and equity, and allows us to be more open and engaged in learning and living so that the world is a better place. Paul Coelho, author of *The Alchemist*, writes, "When we strive to become better than we are, everything around us becomes better too."[1] I used to tell my students that every human on Earth can be better than we are. Each of us can stand to improve in one way or another. Depending on our current ways of being, we might take better care of ourselves, make healthier choices, or show more compassion or respect. The goal of presenting social emotional well-being through a framework is to provide a sustainable system for striving to become better *without* feeling burdened by a passing initiative that is siloed, infeasible, or unmanageable. This framework also helps us to consider six ways of being that align with CASEL's

[1]Paulo Coelho, Alan Clarke, and James Noel Smith, *The Alchemist* (New York: Harper Luxe, 2014).

competencies and personalize them to meet our own needs for personal and professional growth. Much like developing positive character traits, emphasizing *being* more reflective, intentional, empathetic, equitable, connected, and accountable can only enrich our social emotional wellness. Before we break down each aspect of social and emotional well-being, please take a moment to reflect on what it means to you to *be* reflective, intentional, empathetic, connected, accountable, and equitable and what each way of being currently looks like in your life.

To be reflective means:

_____

_____

In my life, *being* reflective looks like (i.e., What type of choices do I make or actions do I take that are reflective?):

_____

_____

To be intentional means:

_____

_____

In my life, *being* intentional looks like:

_____

_____

To be empathetic means:

_____

_____

In my life, *being* empathetic looks like:

_____

_____

To be connected means:

_____

_____

In my life, *being* connected looks like:

_____

_____

To be accountable means:

_____

_____

In my life, *being* accountable looks like:

_____

_____

To be equitable means:

_____

_____

In my life, *being* equitable looks like:

_____

_____

Thank you for taking time to consider your understanding and practice of each way of being. *Being* is a journey. We are all on the journey together. No working in silos, nor waiting for the next best thing. Instead, the pursuit of a way of being through the Framework for Social Emotional Well-Being interweaves the best of a variety of educational initiatives that seek to support adults and students within the school community. As we explore the framework in its entirety, I am certain you will discover connections to social emotional learning, restorative practices, positive school climate, trauma-informed care, and self-care. Before we take a deeper dive into each way of being, I would like to set the stage by introducing three resources we will use to operate the framework: a Tiered Continuum of Questions, the Social Emotional Well-Being Check-In, and the Conscious Connection Chart.

SETTING THE STAGE

A Tiered Continuum of Questions

Most of us who serve students through the educational system, regardless of our roles, have become very familiar with the acronym MTSS, or multi-tiered system of supports. A vast majority of educators have been introduced to MTSS through the lens of positive behavior interventions and supports (PBIS) or response to intervention (RTI)—I know, right back to the acronyms! The reason MTSS is essential in education is that the framework is based in the implementation of science and provides a sustainable process for supporting the academic, behavior, social, or emotional needs of all students to the degree that each student individually necessitates.

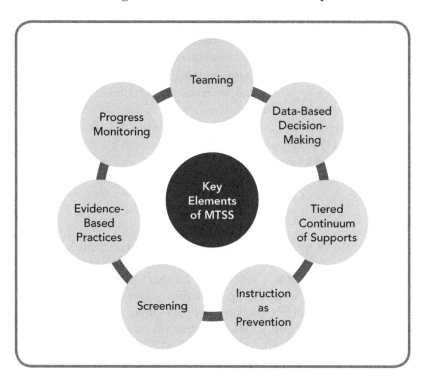

Dr. Ashley Greenwald, an MTSS expert, provides a brief description of a multi-tiered system of supports framework as well as the three-tiered hierarchy component to help you have a basis for understanding before I ask you to join me on a unique exploration of what I will call a Tiered Continuum of Questions. Let's consider Dr. Greenwald's explanation.[1]

---

[1]Ashley Greenwald, written interview response to Michelle L. Trujillo, April 15, 2021.

Multi-tiered systems of support (MTSS) is a framework for organizing support and interventions based on the needs of the population being served. MTSS is often represented in a three-tiered hierarchy of supports that includes assessment, screening, interventions, and monitoring outcomes. MTSS allows for monitoring progress at the level of the individual but also assesses the health of the system.

Sustainability is inherent to MTSS, as one of the core features is teaming. The team builds capacity to implement MTSS and is responsible for ongoing data analysis and action planning. Once the value of MTSS is realized, implementation becomes part of the daily operations of the organization.

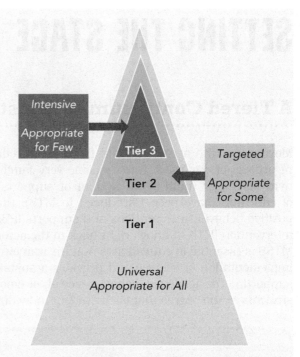

Dr. Ashley Greenwald

While MTSS is much more than a triangle, the three-tiered hierarchy is probably the most recognized feature of MTSS. The hierarchy allows for the organization to build a strong foundation of supports and resources that benefits the entire population, therefore allocating a majority of resources to prevention and the health of the system as a whole. This foundational focus on prevention provides the strength that the system needs to then meet the more unique and personalized needs of the identified population.

I have created a modified version of the tiered-continuum component of MTSS to use as a tool for awareness and potential growth throughout this book. I refer to it as the Tiered Continuum of Questions, and I use it to pose various questions for consideration and reflection at each level. I have always found the three-tiered hierarchy to be a beneficial tool for offering support and providing interventions for students. As I developed the Framework for Social Emotional Well-Being, it occurred to me that using a similar format to ask ourselves questions in an effort to validate some of our behaviors and stimulate consideration for growth or support would be helpful. Thus, each "way of being" section throughout the book includes specific tiered-continuum questions for you to personalize. You will recognize a diagram similar to the one that follows as you journey with me through these pages.

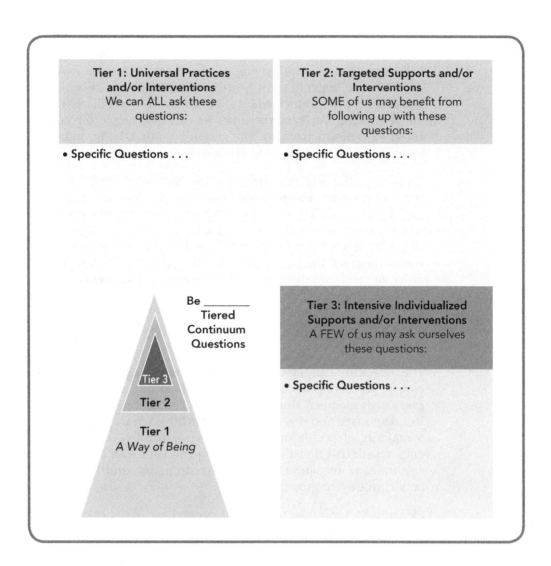

Now, let's delve into another resource that we will use through-out this book and that you can use throughout your life. It is the Social Emotional Well-Being Check-In.

Social Emotional Well-Being Check-In

The Social Emotional Well-Being Check-In is a self-reflection activity that provides individuals with an opportunity to consider thoughts, attitudes, and behaviors that may nourish or neglect one's overall wellness. Please know that the self-reflection check-in is *not* an assessment that we pass or fail. It is simply a tool that is designed to help us to begin to pay attention to how we "be" as we live our daily lives. By contemplating thoughts, attitudes, and behaviors that are challenging versus those that come naturally to us, we can begin to identify areas within our ways of being that cause stress, disconnectedness, or an inadvertent disregard for our well-being. At the same time, we can also begin to recognize those ways in which we live that enrich our mind, body, and spirit; foster our relationships; and promote social responsibility.

Ultimately, the goal is to decrease the number of "very challenging" factors and increase those that are "natural" or "very natural" so that specific areas within our ways of being (the ones with which we struggle or that we neglect) can become more inherent, intrinsic, or intuitive in order to enhance our overall well-being. I have included the check-in in its entirety within this section in order for you to establish a baseline reflection of your current state of being. However, I encourage you to consider using this document to routinely reflect upon your well-being, as it can serve as a resource to promote centering, goal setting, or recognition of accomplishments.

The check-in can also be used to create staffwide goals. Of course, for this purpose it would be filled out anonymously by every staff member. But after doing so, leadership teams can collect responses and determine areas within each way of being that a majority of people on staff practice naturally, as well as the ones most struggle with. The results can establish a platform to celebrate, to recognize whole-group strengths, and to ascertain opportunities for growth.

Please take time now to complete your baseline check-in. Place a mark in the column that best reflects what is true for you in the moment, knowing that your answers are not an indication of good or bad, right or wrong. They are only an indication of where you see yourself to *be* presently. The best part about the check-in is that every time you complete it you may realize something new about yourself, you may begin to notice that ways of being that used to be challenging are becoming more natural, or you may see patterns that cause you to recognize a need for support, knowing that asking for help is a step into courageous vulnerability that, in and of itself, will strengthen your social emotional well-being. Note that you can download a copy of the Social Emotional Well-Being Check-In at **resources.corwin.com/ SocialEmotionalWellBeingforEducators** in order to revisit your check-in periodically or any time you feel it would be helpful to do so.

Baseline Social Emotional Well-Being Check-In

BE REFLECTIVE	VERY CHALLENGING FOR ME	CHALLENGING FOR ME	FAIRLY NATURAL FOR ME	VERY NATURAL FOR ME
I recognize my emotions and feelings with ease.	☐	☐	☐	☐
I consider the root cause of my emotions or feelings.	☐	☐	☐	☐
I contemplate the way in which my emotions physically manifest themselves in my body.	☐	☐	☐	☐
I am aware of the way in which my emotions or feelings may impact the outcome of a life situation.	☐	☐	☐	☐
I consider my attitude first thing each morning.	☐	☐	☐	☐
I consider the impact my attitude, words, and/or behaviors may have on others.	☐	☐	☐	☐
I recognize my strengths of character and vocational talents.	☐	☐	☐	☐
I seek opportunities for personal growth.	☐	☐	☐	☐
I seek opportunities for professional growth.	☐	☐	☐	☐
I recognize when I respond to people or situations from a place of love versus fear.	☐	☐	☐	☐
I am willing to consider and intentionally change my thoughts or ways of being that make assumptions, are judgmental, and/or unintentionally or explicitly express bias.	☐	☐	☐	☐

BE INTENTIONAL	VERY CHALLENGING FOR ME	CHALLENGING FOR ME	FAIRLY NATURAL FOR ME	VERY NATURAL FOR ME
I focus on one task at a time.	☐	☐	☐	☐
I set aside my phone when in the presence of others.	☐	☐	☐	☐
I remember people's names when first introduced.	☐	☐	☐	☐
I am organized and take time to practice stress management techniques.	☐	☐	☐	☐
I let go of situations that are out of my control.	☐	☐	☐	☐
I give myself grace when my plans don't go as I intended.	☐	☐	☐	☐
I leave work *at* work, in order to focus on family, friends, and/or personal responsibilities at home.	☐	☐	☐	☐
I allow myself to try new things, even if failure is likely, in order to learn and grow.	☐	☐	☐	☐
I redirect or walk away from negative conversations.	☐	☐	☐	☐
If I see an unjust situation occur, I say something or do something in an effort to promote justice.	☐	☐	☐	☐
I structure each day so that when my students walk into my class, I can immediately give them my full attention.	☐	☐	☐	☐
When I feel anxious, frustrated, angry, overexcited, or any other emotion that causes my adrenaline to increase, I take at least one intentional breath.	☐	☐	☐	☐
When I feel overwhelmed or frustrated, I calmly let others know how I am feeling and/or request a moment to breathe or refocus.	☐	☐	☐	☐

BE EMPATHETIC	VERY CHALLENGING FOR ME	CHALLENGING FOR ME	FAIRLY NATURAL FOR ME	VERY NATURAL FOR ME
I listen well without thinking about what I want to say in response.	☐	☐	☐	☐
I listen without interrupting, even when I disagree with what is being shared.	☐	☐	☐	☐
In unfamiliar situations, I seek *first* to understand.	☐	☐	☐	☐
I refrain from making judgments about others whose lives and experience may be different from mine.	☐	☐	☐	☐
I am compassionate when someone is in need.	☐	☐	☐	☐
I take the perspective of others to attempt to see situations, ideas, and opinions through their viewpoint.	☐	☐	☐	☐
I read articles and books that inform my understanding of disparities that exist regarding race, ethnicity, gender, ability, religion, and socioeconomic status, especially those that differ from my own.	☐	☐	☐	☐
I initiate conversations with people who have life experiences that differ from mine in an effort to gain insight and understanding.	☐	☐	☐	☐
I engage in restorative practices in an effort to build relationships with others.	☐	☐	☐	☐
I ask, "What happened?" or "Can you tell me more?" as opposed to "Why did you do that?"	☐	☐	☐	☐
I participate in opportunities to serve my community.	☐	☐	☐	☐

BE CONNECTED	VERY CHALLENGING FOR ME	CHALLENGING FOR ME	FAIRLY NATURAL FOR ME	VERY NATURAL FOR ME
I make eye contact with others (if/when appropriate) and greet people by name.	☐	☐	☐	☐
I kinesthetically connect with others when safe and appropriate (i.e., handshake, high five, fist bump, or side hug).	☐	☐	☐	☐
I ask, "How are you?" and stop to look at the person as I listen to their answer.	☐	☐	☐	☐
I seek to understand the story behind the customs, traditions, and ways of being of others.	☐	☐	☐	☐
I establish healthy relationships that enrich my social emotional well-being.	☐	☐	☐	☐
I maintain healthy relationships that enrich my social emotional well-being.	☐	☐	☐	☐
I communicate well with others.	☐	☐	☐	☐
I willingly collaborate and work well with others.	☐	☐	☐	☐
I practice random acts of kindness.	☐	☐	☐	☐
I offer assistance without hesitation when a student, colleague, or friend needs support or help.	☐	☐	☐	☐
I offer assistance without hesitation when a stranger with whom I cross paths needs support or help.	☐	☐	☐	☐
I share my vocational passion, talents, and interests with others.	☐	☐	☐	☐
I demonstrate respect for others by listening well and honoring their views and perspectives.	☐	☐	☐	☐
I take time to get to know others by showing interest in their endeavors and asking them to share their life or learning experiences.	☐	☐	☐	☐

BE ACCOUNTABLE	VERY CHALLENGING FOR ME	CHALLENGING FOR ME	FAIRLY NATURAL FOR ME	VERY NATURAL FOR ME
I make responsible decisions.	☐	☐	☐	☐
I am reliable.	☐	☐	☐	☐
I make time to exercise at least three days per week in order to attend to my physical well-being.	☐	☐	☐	☐
I seek support when necessary to nourish my mental and/or emotional well-being.	☐	☐	☐	☐
I set boundaries that support my social emotional well-being.	☐	☐	☐	☐
I engage in at least one behavior per week that nurtures my spiritual well-being, such as praying, meditating, being in nature, or attending a religious ceremony.	☐	☐	☐	☐
I consider the impact of my choices on others when I make decisions.	☐	☐	☐	☐
I am culturally aware and responsive in my vocational practice.	☐	☐	☐	☐
I am ethically aware and responsive in my vocational practice.	☐	☐	☐	☐
I follow rules or protocols without exception.	☐	☐	☐	☐
I sincerely and verbally take responsibility for choices I make that negatively impact myself or others.	☐	☐	☐	☐
I seek sincere forgiveness when my words, attitudes, or behaviors negatively impact another.	☐	☐	☐	☐
I do the right thing, even when no one is watching.	☐	☐	☐	☐
I make a concerted effort to respond to situations from a place of love, as opposed to fear.	☐	☐	☐	☐
I take a stand against inequity and injustice.	☐	☐	☐	☐

BE EQUITABLE	VERY CHALLENGING FOR ME	CHALLENGING FOR ME	FAIRLY NATURAL FOR ME	VERY NATURAL FOR ME
I recognize my own explicit biases.	☐	☐	☐	☐
I recognize my own implicit biases.	☐	☐	☐	☐
I honor and respect the language, customs, and cultural norms of others.	☐	☐	☐	☐
I understand historical and systemic inequities based on race, ethnicity, gender, ability, religion, socioeconomic status, and more.	☐	☐	☐	☐
I respectfully engage in conversations with others whose cultural experiences differ from my own in order to learn, grow, and act in a fair and impartial manner.	☐	☐	☐	☐
I notice and respectfully confront injustice and/or inequities.	☐	☐	☐	☐
I set high expectations and provide high support for *all* students (and staff).	☐	☐	☐	☐
I consider the needs of *all* students (or staff) when designing instruction or making decisions.	☐	☐	☐	☐
I differentiate instruction or activities to meet the needs of *all* learners.	☐	☐	☐	☐
I consider accessibility barriers and make necessary modifications when assigning tasks or homework.	☐	☐	☐	☐
I create opportunities to learn about the customs, traditions, and ways of being of others.	☐	☐	☐	☐

The final resource that I would like to introduce before we dive deeper into each way of being is the Conscious Connection Chart.

Conscious Connection Chart

Often in the context of social emotional learning, we are asked to identify our emotions (self-awareness) and to regulate those emotions (self-management) in a given situation so that they help, rather than hinder, life experiences. My colleagues Lori Nathanson and Kori Hamilton Biagas and I have designed a process to assist in helping people to operationalize the identification and regulation of emotions. In consideration of Dr. Stephen Porges's Polyvagal theory, we suggest that, in order to experience enhanced social emotional well-being, it is necessary to identify the way in which we respond to life situations. Typically, humans respond in one of three ways: We spike into high alert by way of fight or flight, we ride the waves and maintain our balance, or we go into total shutdown by freezing and collapsing into ourselves or onto others.

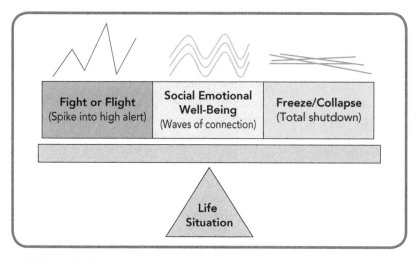

©2021 K. Hamilton Biagas, L. Nathanson, and M. Trujillo

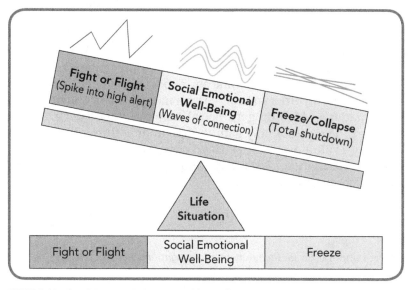

©2021 K. Hamilton Biagas, L. Nathanson, and M. Trujillo

Riding the waves and finding a sense of balance that enriches our well-being is the ultimate goal. We realize this is easier said than done, yet the reality is that, in order to cultivate our social emotional well-being, it is necessary to identify subtle physiological responses to life situations, our emotions and feelings that develop from these responses, and the external behaviors that can ultimately ensue. Additionally, recognizing specific strategies, both conscious and unconscious, that can impact the outcome of a situation may be the key to finding balance.

It's really about balance. Some life circumstances, such as the toxic stress of poverty or other forms of trauma, send us into survival mode—fight, flight, or freeze—and it's easy to feel stuck. And yet, even in these situations, people find the joy, love, or curiosity to thrive! Finding our way back to riding the waves of connection, even for a moment, can help bring us back into balance and start to retone our nervous systems.

For me, as someone who has dealt with depression, practicing and teaching yoga—a mind–body practice—is one constant that helps me tune into myself and connect with others so that, rather than getting stuck, I find balance in nurturing my social emotional well-being.

Dr. Lori Nathanson

More specifically, when we experience a challenging life situation or ongoing stress, it generally manifests itself physiologically or as a subtle internal response that stimulates our emotions or feelings. Emotions and feelings can be puzzling because although we often use them interchangeably they are, in fact, different. Dr. Nathanson explains, "Labeling is one way of making emotions into conscious feelings. Naming or labeling an emotion brings it into our awareness, adding a layer of processing that may transform it into longer-lasting feelings."[2] Furthermore, when we intentionally reflect upon the external behaviors precipitated from our emotions or feelings, we become aware of our ability to consciously make a choice in order to experience a more positive outcome from life situations. According to social-cognitive theorist Dr. Albert Bandura, "People not only gain understanding through reflection, but they evaluate and alter their own thinking."[3] For example, given two scenarios, observe the difference in the impact on our social emotional well-being:

---

[2]Lori Nathanson, interview by Michelle L. Trujillo, July 13, 2021.

[3]Albert Bandura, *Social Foundations of Thought and Action: A Social Cognitive Theory* (New York: Prentice Hall, 1986), 21.

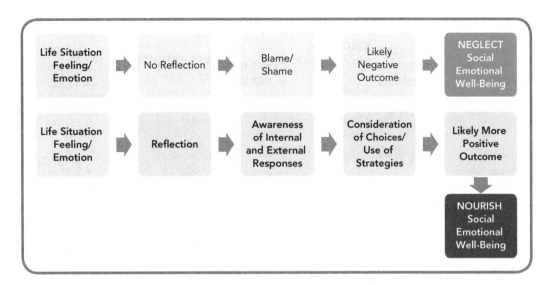

At the same time, awareness is just the first step. The Conscious Connection Chart that follows helps us to make connections between life situations and potential outcomes by presenting possible feelings/emotions, internal responses, and external behaviors that may occur in the chasm between the situation and the outcome. Consider the chart for a moment and identify the various examples we have provided. Note that the examples are just that. They are not set in stone, nor are they absolute. My colleagues and I merely want to provide you with an exemplar from which to personalize, learn, compare, and connect.

Conscious Connection Chart

LIFE SITUATION	INTERNAL/ SUBTLE RESPONSES (What this can feel like inside)	EMOTIONS (Unconscious or conscious response) / FEELINGS (Conscious, labeling)	EXTERNAL BEHAVIORS (What this can look like)	STRATEGIES (Unconscious or conscious choices we can make)	POTENTIAL OUTCOME
Red Zone **FIGHT OR FLIGHT** (Spikes)	Heart rate increases Potential cortisol release Blood flow increases to limbs Heart races or flutters	Frustrated Angry Enraged Worried Anxious Fearful Panicked	Yell/scream Tense up Sweat Clench (jaw, fists) Quick movements Jittery	*Unconscious/ conscious choice:* Being defensive Blaming Avoidance Running away	Get into fights Vocational insecurity Relationship conflict Isolation

(Continued)

(Continued)

LIFE SITUATION	INTERNAL/ SUBTLE RESPONSES (What this can feel like inside)	EMOTIONS (Unconscious or conscious response) / FEELINGS (Conscious, labeling)	EXTERNAL BEHAVIORS (What this can look like)	STRATEGIES (Unconscious or conscious choices we can make)	POTENTIAL OUTCOME
Green Zone **SOCIAL EMOTIONAL WELL-BEING** (Waves)	Steady heart rate Potential dopamine, serotonin, and/or oxytocin release	Joyous Curious Present Safe Happy Calm Hopeful Peaceful	Smile Laughter Asking questions Focused Relaxed Energetic Moving with purpose	Conscious choice of being _____. (way of being)	Personal or professional growth Healthy relationships Improved student engagement
Blue Zone **FREEZE** (Collapse, flat)	Heavy limbs Heightened levels of cortisol	Helpless Sad Depressed Discouraged Numb Shut down	Flat affect Exhausted Moving away (physically) Fainting	*Unconscious/ conscious choice:* Apathy Complacency Doing nothing Indecision	Vocational overwhelmingness Mental/emotional fatigue Isolation Compromised immunity

©2021 K. Hamilton Biagas, L. Nathanson, and M. Trujillo

What differences do you see when you compare the *Social Emotional Well-Being* row with the *Fight/Flight* and *Freeze* rows? If you consider your state of being when life situations are complicated, on which row do you see yourself? What about when all seems to be going your way, when your days seem smooth and enjoyable?

Having considered those questions, here is another one for us to consider: Why do some people tend to consistently find themselves living life in the green zone, while others tend to bounce between red and blue more often than not? To some degree, it may be our personalities, our family dynamics, or our various life experiences. At the same time, these tendencies can also be specifically related to the systemic inequities that are prevalent in society, as well as within the educational system. There are people among us who live in poverty, people who live with less stability and opportunity, and people who experience racism or other biases on a consistent basis. And of these people, many are of color. Reflecting on the Conscious Connection Chart, we recognize that many of our students find themselves living in the green zones, while others remain rooted in the red zones of the chart. Consider Kori Hamilton Biagas's perspective.[4]

---

[4]Kori Hamilton Biagas, written interview response to Michelle L. Trujillo, July 15, 2021.

Many of our students experience "hardship" in ways that are created and sustained through systems that disproportionately increase unjust and inequitable experiences.

These ongoing experiences, of which our students have little to no control, shape the way they view and interact with the people they encounter, including their classmates and teachers. Yet some are able to acquire and refine the skills needed to both navigate and, at times, thrive in these situations, while others push through in survival mode.

Kori Hamilton Biagas

At the same time, no matter who we are—the color of our skin or our life's circumstances—it is healthier for our mind, body, and spirit to live in the space of social emotional well-being as opposed to fight, flight, or freeze. And the best part about this is that—whether we believe it or not—in many cases we have more control than we think over which zone we end up functioning within. I know this all too well, so let me use myself as an example. Take a look at two different scenarios from a morning in my life as an educator:

Scenario One:

- I awake at 4:45 a.m. because I left so much work on my desk. I feel like I can't breathe.

- I take a quick shower, rush to get dressed, attempt to straighten my hair, which doesn't go well because I didn't take enough time to dry it, and grab coffee as I bolt out the door.

- I spill my coffee in the car because, in my rush, I didn't secure my lid. I want to scream.

- I get to work, looking forward to an hour alone before anyone else arrives. When I step out of my car, I notice that one of my colleagues—one who likes to talk—has arrived before me and will likely show up in my classroom just as I sit at my desk.

- And there he is. I hold my breath and greet him with restrained frustration.

- I don't have time to greet my students as they arrive for first period because I have too many papers to grade and emails left unanswered; if I can just get a few off my plate, I know I will feel better.

- Yet just before the tardy bell rings, I hear one student yell across the room at another (something about his mother!), and I sprint to intervene before all chaos erupts.

- I am just beginning class when I get a call from the office, reminding me that I have not yet taken roll. Really? Who has time to take roll?

Scenario Two:

- I awake at 6:00 a.m. I realize that I left work on my desk yesterday, but I also know that I need a good night's sleep to function as a decent human being during the day.

(Continued)

(Continued)

- I turn on my music as I shower, dress, and do my hair. I love starting the morning with music! It makes me feel happy.

- I arrive at work about the same time as most of my colleagues, and we visit as we walk in from the parking lot.

- There isn't enough time to get started on my work left over from yesterday, so I take a deep breath and write myself a reminder note to set boundaries during my prep period by staying in my room to grade papers and respond to email.

- I stand outside my door as the first bell rings and greet students by name as they enter my room. I try to give a high five or fist bump and make a point to recognize each student with a positive comment. Their responses make my heart smile.

- As students settle into their desks, I ask them to turn to a neighbor and share one word that represents fun, while I take roll and smile as I hear "no school," "skateboarding," and "hanging out with my brother."

- I begin class by calling out a few responses I overheard, and then I direct them to today's lesson.

Thank you for walking through these two diverse but genuine examples from my life in the classroom. My husband, who is my best friend and my greatest accountability partner, will tell you that I spent a good portion of my career as a teacher and an administrator in the red zone, functioning in a rushed state. Although building relationships with students and growing the community within my classroom or school was always a priority to me, I still struggled with managing my time well, taking care of myself, and slowing down long enough to breathe. Even today, I find myself living in the red zone far too often. Fortunately, my husband calls me on my stuff! In fact, one of the reasons that I created the Framework for Social Emotional Well-Being is that I need awareness, practice, and accountability every day! I strive to cultivate my social emotional well-being daily, and the reality is that I often fail to achieve green-zone status. Yet educators know well that failure is a valuable teacher. As such, I continue to learn from each moment as I seek to find balance within the zones.

As you contemplate the Conscious Connection Chart and my two scenarios, which scenario better represents your typical morning? Could you create a scenario from a day in your vocational life? What might it look like if the ultimate outcome neglected your social emotional well-being (red and/or blue zone)? What would it look like if your social emotional well-being was nourished (green zone)? Feel free to create your own scenarios and then use the blank Conscious Connection Chart to fill in your potential reality in each column for the green, red, and blue zone.

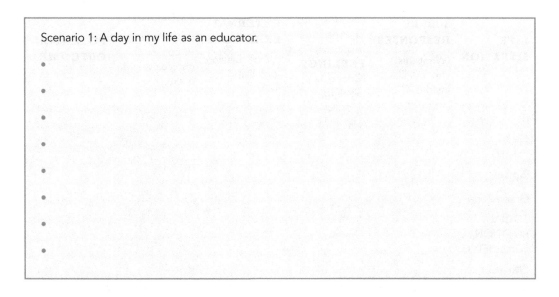

Scenario 1: A day in my life as an educator.

-
-
-
-
-
-
-
-

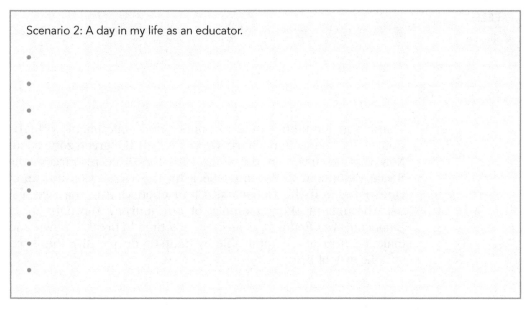

Scenario 2: A day in my life as an educator.

-
-
-
-
-
-
-
-
-

As you fill in each box of the Conscious Connection Chart, focus on the emotions and feelings column. Please use as many descriptive words to identify potential emotions and feelings that you can think that align with each of your scenarios. Feel free to use slang or vernacular that is most familiar to you. Fill in the remaining columns, as you wish, again using experiences that are known to you.

Conscious Connection Chart

LIFE SITUATION	INTERNAL/ SUBTLE RESPONSES (What this can feel like inside)	EMOTIONS (Unconscious or conscious response) / FEELINGS (Conscious, labeling)	EXTERNAL BEHAVIORS (What this can look like)	STRATEGIES (Unconscious or conscious choices we can make)	POTENTIAL OUTCOME
Red Zone: FIGHT OR FLIGHT (Spikes)					
Green Zone: SOCIAL EMOTIONAL WELL-BEING (Waves)					
Blue Zone: FREEZE (Collapse, flat)					

©2021 K. Hamilton Biagas, L. Nathanson, and M. Trujillo

Thank you for taking time to ponder and experiment with the Conscious Connection Chart. We will revisit the green zone soon. Now that we have set the stage with the three resources—the Social Emotional Well-Being Check-In, the Tiered Continuum of Questions, and the Conscious Connection Chart—that we will use throughout the remainder of our journey through *Social Emotional Well-Being for Educators*, it's time to break it down and make each resource applicable by taking a deeper dive into each specific way of being.

A DEEPER DIVE

RELEVANCE, RECOGNITION, REFLECTION, AND MAKING IT REAL

Framework for Social Emotional Well-Being

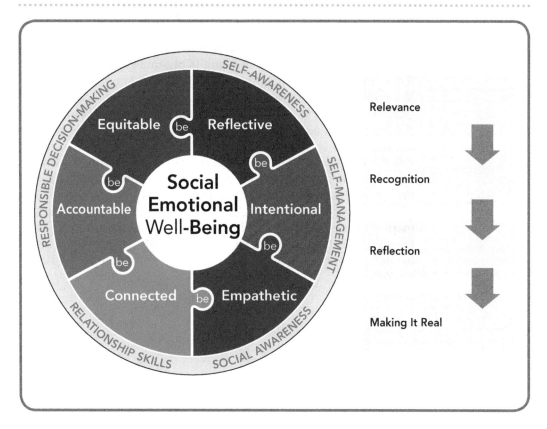

As you know, the Framework for Social Emotional Well-Being is based on six ways of being:

- Be Reflective
- Be Intentional
- Be Empathetic

- Be Connected

- Be Accountable

- Be Equitable

I chose to focus on these specific fundamentals because each way of being is essential to improving our quality of life as everyday human beings *and* each is particularly relevant and applicable to our vocational practice as educators. More specifically, because school districts across the nation are using the social emotional learning competencies as defined by CASEL to teach skills that support the well-being of both students and adults, each chosen way of being within the Framework for Social Emotional Well-Being is naturally associated with a specific competency. Therefore, aligned professional learning and student instruction can be implemented with continuity and clarity.

As we embark on our deeper dive, know that an entire book could be exclusively dedicated to each separate way of being. I have chosen instead to present key concepts, pertinent guidance, and essential questions based on my experience as an educator. Furthermore, please note that each way of being is organized into four areas of focus: Relevance, Recognition, Reflection, and Making It Real. The *Relevance* portion is designed to present a concise common language and understanding for each respective way of being within the framework, as well as to draw a direct link to why focusing on the particular way of being is relevant to enriching your own personal and professional social emotional wellness. The *Recognition* segment is designed to provide you with an opportunity to recognize your strengths, while the *Reflection* portion allows you room to explore opportunities for growth. Finally, the *Making It Real* segment presents two options that can be used to intentionally reinforce and cultivate your social emotional well-being. Are you ready to explore, learn, and grow? Let's dive in to our first way of being: Be Reflective.

BE REFLECTIVE

Being reflective is likely one of the most growth-based ways of being that can positively impact our own lives and the lives of those with whom we interact, care for, and love. Although most of us would acknowledge that some the best educators are those who are reflective, I think we would also acknowledge that it is a challenge to be reflective. Sometimes, I wonder if it is just human nature. As human beings we are inclined to protect ourselves—from shame, doubt, uncertainty, failure, recrimination, criticism, you name it! We create protective shields in a variety of ways. Some of us get defensive, others blame. Sometimes, we erect walls or slam doors. At other times, we isolate or run.

None of these shields, however, cultivate our social emotional well-being, which is why being reflective is paramount. Granted, being reflective takes courageous vulnerability. It calls us to look inward before we speak, teach, or point toward those outside of ourselves. Being reflective requires grace toward ourselves first and foremost. It is a humbling experience because as we begin to be reflective we are likely to find areas within our lives that we can grow or improve. Being reflective can also create cause for celebration. Being reflective can illuminate strengths, confirm convictions, and reinforce behavior. Thus, to be reflective is to be self-aware. Ultimately, when we practice being reflective, we are apt to find our best selves, as humans who are willing to look within in order to grow out.

BE REFLECTIVE

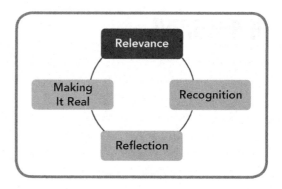

WHAT does it mean and look like to Be Reflective?

Being reflective means looking within. The primary focus includes, but is not limited to these actions:

- Contemplating our vocational why

- Noticing our emotions or feelings, as well as the physical manifestations and potential root causes of our feelings

- Acknowledging that emotions are neither good or bad, right or wrong—they just are

- Noticing the connections between our thoughts, attitudes, and ways of behavior

- Recognizing our strengths, talents, and/or skills

- Considering opportunities that will foster personal and professional growth

- Noticing thoughts that lead to assumptions, judgments, or biases

WHY is it relevant to social emotional well-being?

- *Personal Relevance*: Being reflective leads to personal growth. We cannot grow from that which we ignore, nor can we leverage a strength without recognizing it.

- *Professional Relevance*: The ability to be reflective can help us to connect or reconnect with the purpose and meaning of our vocations, thus inspiring joy, confidence, effectiveness, and productivity.

SEL Connection: Self-Awareness

BE REFLECTIVE

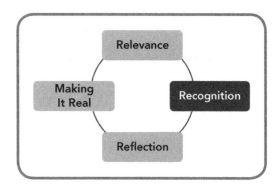

Regardless of my role as an educator—teacher, principal, or educational consultant—I have found a strengths-based approach to school climate, classroom instruction, solution seeking, or professional growth to be much more productive and effective than a deficit model. Thus, as we lean into the pursuit of each way of being, I would like to ask you to first recognize strengths you possess that can be leveraged to nourish your social emotional well-being. Let's revisit the Be Reflective section of the Social Emotional Well-Being Check-In. Please take a moment to highlight one or two statements that stand out to you as personal or vocational strengths. Also, feel free to add a strength or two that are not listed at the bottom of the self-reflection check-in.

BE REFLECTIVE
I recognize my emotions and feelings with ease.
I consider the root cause of my emotions or feelings.
I contemplate the way in which my emotions physically manifest themselves in my body.
I am aware of the way in which my emotions or feelings may impact the outcome of a life situation.
I consider my attitude first thing each morning.
I consider the impact that my attitude, words, and/or behaviors may have on others.
I recognize my strengths of character and vocational talents.
I seek opportunities for personal growth.
I seek opportunities for professional growth.
I recognize when I respond to people or situations from a place of love versus fear.
I am willing to consider and intentionally change my thoughts or ways of being that make assumptions, are judgmental, and/or unintentionally or explicitly express bias.

Considering the row or two that you highlighted, or a strength you may have added, what does the practice of this way of being look like in your life?

_____

_____

_____

_____

How might the practice of your highlighted strength or strengths positively impact your well-being?

_____

_____

_____

_____

How might the practice of your highlighted strength or strengths positively impact those with whom you interact, care for, or love?

_____

_____

_____

_____

How might you leverage at least one of these strengths in order to provide an opportunity for another to feel valued or appreciated?

_____

_____

_____

_____

Thank you for taking time to recognize your personal and vocational strengths. You may find it helpful, as we journey through each way of being, to revisit your strengths and to ask yourself how you might reframe a challenge or opportunity for growth by leveraging your strengths. Thus, as we move into the *Reflection* segment, please keep your strengths at the forefront of your heart and mind.

BE REFLECTIVE

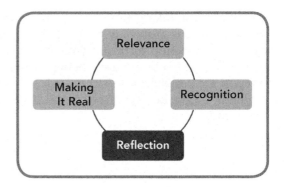

As you are aware, there are two resources within *Social Emotional Well-Being for Educators* that will provide you with opportunities to reflect your thoughts, words, and behaviors regarding each way of being within the framework: the Social Emotional Well-Being Check-In and the Tiered Continuum of Questions. We will use these resources as we step into the reflection portion of our process to promote social emotional well-being. It is very deliberate that the first way of being that we will reflect on is Be Reflective. I hope you appreciate the intentional irony!

Academic philosopher and proponent of educational reform, John Dewey, shared this wisdom more than a century ago: "We do not learn from experience. . . . We learn from reflecting on experience."[1] Reflection causes us to consider what is working well and what isn't. Reflection creates space for us to wonder and learn. Thus, a powerful tool for reflection is curiosity. Consider what it means to be curious for a moment. Three-year-old children can be our best examples of the curious mind. They ask "why" about everything! They ask because they are trying to figure out the world they live in, as well as their place in it. Sometimes, I wonder if, as we age, our chronological wisdom depletes our sense of discovery. If you agree that this might be true for you, I encourage you to reach back into your childhood and grab hold of the curiosity you possessed then. Begin by asking yourself why you do what you do. As educators, we know well that *what* we do lacks meaning and purpose unless we know *why* we do it. So it is time to start asking ourselves questions about our thoughts, attitudes, words, and behaviors. It is time to invest in being reflective. Please take a moment to stop reading and flip back to pp. 25–30 to review your baseline answers on the Social Emotional Learning Check-In for the Be Reflective section. Reflect for a minute on why you answered the way you did. Keep your answers in mind as you consider the forthcoming Tiered Continuum of Questions.

---

[1]Suzie Boss, "PBL Teachers Need Time to Reflect, Too," *Edutopia*, George Lucas Educational Foundation, November 28, 2012, www.edutopia.org/blog/project-learning-teacher-reflection-suzie-boss.

Here are a few suggestions before you begin. As you contemplate the continuum, focus first on the triangle as a whole. Notice that there is a collective way of being emphasized in the green portion at the base of the triangle that sets a foundation for the continuum. Remember that Tier 1/green-level questions are universal; they are questions every one of us can ask ourselves. Best practice suggests that we consistently ask ourselves these questions, as our answers may change based on any moment in time, new experience, or challenging situation. Based on our answers, some of us may want to consider the questions listed at the Tier 2/blue level, and the same is true for the Tier 3/purple-level questions, which a few of us may want to reflect upon. Keep in mind that these are simply questions to encourage you to think about your way of being in the context of being reflective. An answer of yes or no does not indicate good or bad, healthy or unhealthy, "got it all together" or "struggling to survive." Your answers simply give you information with which to make choices, if you so choose. There should be no pressure or concern about right or wrong. Merely read through the questions, sit with your authentic answers for a bit, and then feel free to process through the question prompts, the Guided Reflection Flowchart options, and/or the journaling space at the end of the section.

Be Reflective
Tiered Continuum
Self-Reflection Questions

Tier 1: Universal Practices
We can ALL ask these questions:

- Do I understand what it means to Be Reflective?
- Am I conscientious of recognizing or noticing my own emotions?
- Do I notice when my emotions are physically manifested in my body language or body response?
- Have I taken time to contemplate my character strengths and vocational talents? If so, can I list three? If not, am I willing to take time to reflect on my strengths?
- Am I intentional about coming from a place of love, as opposed to fear, in my approach to people and situations?
- Am I willing to consider areas in which I would benefit from personal and/or professional growth?
  - If so, am I willing to evaluate potential areas in which I demonstrate implicit bias?
- Do I contemplate my own understanding, or lack thereof, of social identities regarding race, class, gender, nationality, family structure, and how each contributes to one's sense of power and agency in various contexts?

Tier 2: Targeted Support and/or Intervention
Some of us may benefit from following up with these questions:

- Would it help to talk to another person or people whom I trust in order to learn to recognize my emotions or my strengths?
- Would I benefit from small-group support/work to focus on areas in which I desire to grow?
  - If so, what would that look like? Who might I reach out to for support?
- Do my implicit biases show up explicitly and might a workshop, training, or course help me to be more self-aware?
- Do I acknowledge that I have more to learn regarding social, racial, or cultural identities?
  - If so, what steps will I take to learn and grow? For example, what will I read and/or from whom will I seek guidance and information?

Tier 3: Intensive Individualized Support and/or Intervention
A FEW of us may ask ourselves:

- Does my lack of *being* reflective cause me to engage in self-destructive behaviors?
- When I finally become aware of my emotions, do I feel I am "past the point of no return"?
- Do I believe that I am without strengths?
  - If I answered YES to any of the above questions, might it help to seek the support of a counselor, psychologist, or psychiatrist to become healthier and more self-aware?

BE REFLECTIVE

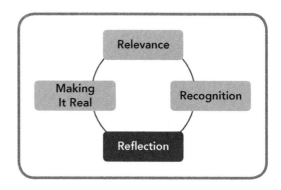

Please use the following question prompts to reflect upon your personal and professional awareness and practice of being reflective. I have worded the prompts in the first person so that you can personalize each answer as you process your reflections.

What do I notice about myself?

_____

_____

_____

_____

Were there any questions that were difficult for me to answer? If so, why?

_____

_____

_____

_____

Did my answers surprise me in any way? If so, why?

_____

_____

_____

_____

(Continued)

(Continued)

Is there anything else that occurs to me as I reflect upon what *being reflective* looks like, feels like, or means in my life?

_____

_____

_____

_____

The Guided Reflection Flowchart is a visual template designed to provide you with a process to intentionally consider and potentially apply action to specific Tiered Continuum Questions. I have chosen a question for you to use as an example in the Guided Flowchart, but I have also provided you with a template to choose your own question, as well as a blank page to create your own flow. Please feel free to use the template that best appeals to your style of learning and growing. Also, this flowchart and its template can be downloaded at **resources.corwin.com/SocialEmotionalWellBeingforEducators** for your ease and accessibility.

Guided Reflection Flowchart Template

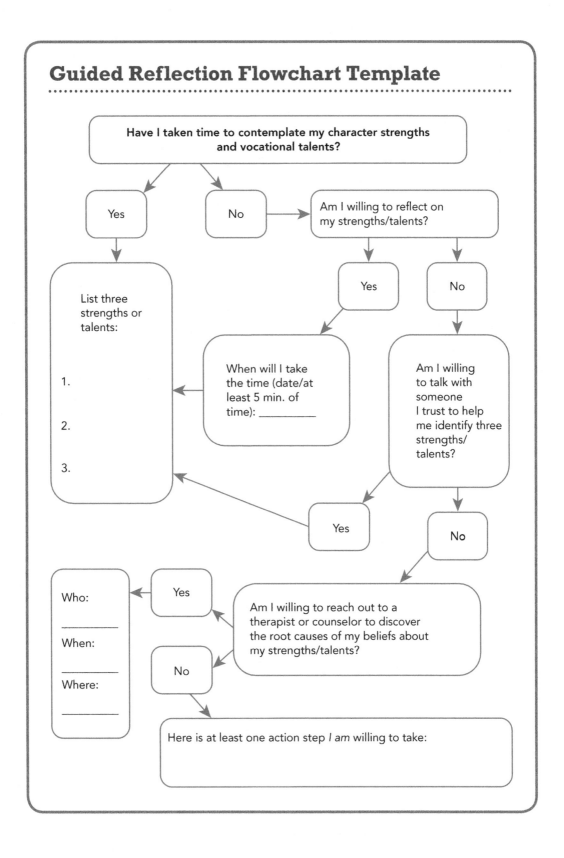

Have I taken time to contemplate my character strengths and vocational talents?

Yes

No → Am I willing to reflect on my strengths/talents?

Yes

No

List three strengths or talents:

1.

2.

3.

When will I take the time (date/at least 5 min. of time): _____

Am I willing to talk with someone I trust to help me identify three strengths/talents?

Yes

No

Who:
_____
When:
_____
Where:
_____

Yes

No

Am I willing to reach out to a therapist or counselor to discover the root causes of my beliefs about my strengths/talents?

Here is at least one action step *I am* willing to take:

Reflection Flowchart Template

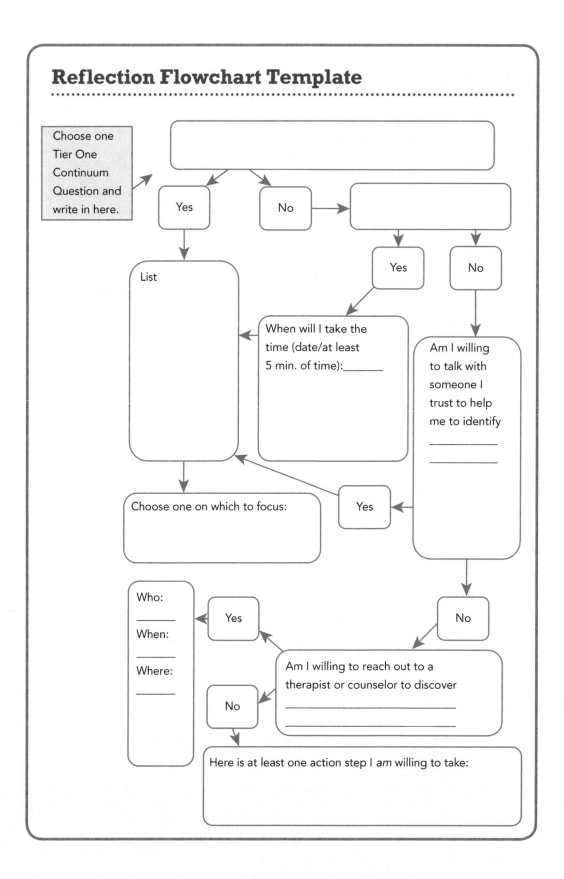

Choose one Tier One Continuum Question and write in here.

Yes

No

Yes

No

List

When will I take the time (date/at least 5 min. of time):_____

Am I willing to talk with someone I trust to help me to identify

_____
_____

Choose one on which to focus:

Yes

Who:
_____
When:
_____
Where:
_____

Yes

No

Am I willing to reach out to a therapist or counselor to discover

_____
_____

No

Here is at least one action step I *am* willing to take:

Reflection Flowchart: Create Your Own

BE REFLECTIVE

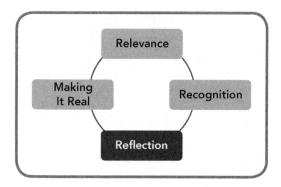

Journaling Opportunity: Feel free to use the space below to write out any thoughts, reminders, "ahas," or curiosities that have occurred to you throughout the *Reflection* segment.

_____

_____

_____

_____

_____

_____

_____

_____

_____

_____

_____

_____

_____

_____

_____

_____

BE REFLECTIVE

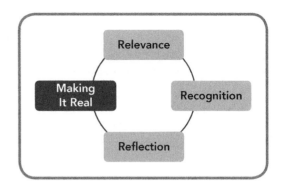

If you chose to use the flowchart options or to journal your reflections, you may have noticed an area in your life in which you have an opportunity for growth regarding your awareness or practice of being reflective. Upon reflection, all of us should be able to identify at least one way in which we would like to improve or be more attentive. If not, we may want to spend a little more time being reflective! All kidding aside, in order to nurture and sustain a healthy social emotional well-being, it is essential that we cultivate opportunities to grow, develop, or improve within each way of being. A mindset focused on growth can expand one's self-efficacy, enhance relationships, and foster personal and professional aptitudes. Thus, I ask you to make it real by accepting my Cultivation Challenge. This challenge is an experience that you can take on individually, or it can be accepted as a small-group or whole-staff encounter. The goal of the Cultivation Challenge is to engage in a process to cultivate positive change. Within this challenge, we will learn to reverse engineer a section of the Conscious Connection Chart in order to create outcomes that will highlight strategies, external behaviors, internal responses, and feelings or emotions that will enrich our social emotional well-being. Ready? Let's do this!

Cultivation Challenge: Making It Real in Three, Two, One!

Three: Answer these three questions. (*Note*: Change "I" to "we" if accepting this challenge as a group.)

1. What is one area in which I have an opportunity for growth regarding my awareness or practice of being reflective?

_____

_____

(Continued)

(Continued)

2. Why did I choose this area for growth?

_____

_____

_____

_____

_____

_____

3. If I were to grow or improve in this area, what would it make possible in my personal and/or professional life?

_____

_____

_____

_____

_____

_____

Two: List at least two ideas or ways that I might cultivate my opportunity for growth.

1. _____

_____

_____

2. _____

_____

_____

One: Choose one idea to apply. Use the Growth Action Plan table to record one idea, practice, and track and then celebrate or revise that idea or way to cultivate growth.

1. Growth Action Plan

OPPORTUNITY FOR GROWTH	PRACTICE	TRACK	CELEBRATE OR REVISE
List one idea or way to cultivate growth.	List one internal (thought/attitude) and one external (words, behaviors) element to practice.	Set a tangible goal for the week and tally the times per day you engage in practice.	Record a star or checkmark at the end of the week if your goal is met or revise your goal to scaffold your practice if necessary.
1.	1.	Goal:	Celebrate:
	2.	Tally:	Revise:

Conscious Connection Challenge

Please take a moment to revisit the green-zone section of the Conscious Connection Chart.

LIFE SITUATION	INTERNAL/ SUBTLE RESPONSES (What this can feel like inside)	EMOTIONS (Unconscious response) / FEELINGS (Conscious, labeling)	EXTERNAL BEHAVIORS (What this can look like)	STRATEGIES (Unconscious or conscious choices we can make to Be Reflective)	POTENTIAL OUTCOME
Green Zone SOCIAL EMOTIONAL WELL-BEING					

(Continued)

(Continued)

In order to apply our Conscious Connection Challenge, we will change the wording of the last column, "Potential Outcome," to "Desired Outcome." The purpose is to operationalize the chart so that we can experience the power of making conscious, proactive choices that are more likely to lead to the desired outcome of enriching our well-being—as opposed to reverting to a reactive mode, often resulting in flight, fight, or freeze, which can diminish or encumber our social, emotional, physical, and/or spiritual health. The way we will implement this chart is through a process called reverse engineering. The idea of reverse engineering is to determine a desired outcome and then work backward in order to establish tangible strategies and behaviors, as well as recognize emotions and internal responses that enhance our social emotional well-being. Ultimately, accepting the Conscious Connection Challenge by reverse engineering for a desired outcome will illuminate possibilities.

You will notice within the process, I use words like "would," "could," and "may" because the goal is to open our hearts and minds to what we might make possible if we choose to make a conscious choice within a specific way of being. Also, keep in mind that the chart is meant to be applied to *our* lives—what we experience, think, say, or do—although the outcome likely represents a *connection* between our own lives and those of others. Let me define the process and give you an example.

Give a specific Life Situation: _____

Step 1: Determine a desired outcome you would like to achieve in your personal or professional life.

Step 2: Define one conscious choice you *could* make in the realm of a specific way of being **reflective** in order to achieve your desired outcome.

Step 3: Explain what it might look like if the outcome were to be achieved.

Step 4: List two to three emotions or feeling words that may be experienced if outcome were to be achieved.

Step 5: List one or two internal or subtle responses that may be present if outcome were to be achieved.

	END STEP 5	STEP 4	STEP 3	STEP 2	START STEP 1
LIFE SITUATION	INTERNAL/ SUBTLE RESPONSES (What this feels like inside)	EMOTIONS / FEELINGS (What we experience based on emotions)	EXTERNAL BEHAVIORS (What this looks like)	STRATEGIES (A conscious choice we make to Be Reflective)	DESIRED OUTCOME
Green Zone SOCIAL EMOTIONAL WELL-BEING					

Example

Life Situation: A student is apathetic about learning and is disruptive in class.

	END STEP 5	STEP 4	STEP 3	STEP 2	START STEP 1
LIFE SITUATION	INTERNAL/ SUBTLE RESPONSES (What this can feel like inside)	EMOTIONS/ FEELINGS (What we experience based on emotions)	EXTERNAL BEHAVIORS (What this can look like)	STRATEGIES (A conscious choice we make to Be Reflective)	DESIRED OUTCOME
Green Zone SOCIAL EMOTIONAL WELL-BEING					I want my student to care about her studies and engage respectfully in class discussions and activities.

	END STEP 5	STEP 4	STEP 3	STEP 2	START STEP 1
LIFE SITUATION	INTERNAL/ SUBTLE RESPONSES (What this can feel like inside)	EMOTIONS/ FEELINGS (What we experience based on emotions)	EXTERNAL BEHAVIORS (What this can look like)	STRATEGIES (A conscious choice we make to Be Reflective)	DESIRED OUTCOME
Green Zone SOCIAL EMOTIONAL WELL-BEING				I will acknowledge that I may have made assumptions about this student, and I will create opportunities to get to know her better.	I want my student to care about her studies and engage respectfully in class discussions and activities.

(Continued)

(Continued)

	END STEP 5	STEP 4	STEP 3	STEP 2	START STEP 1
LIFE SITUATION	INTERNAL/ SUBTLE RESPONSES (What this can feel like inside)	EMOTIONS/ FEELINGS (What we experience based on emotions)	EXTERNAL BEHAVIORS (What this can look like)	STRATEGIES (A conscious choice we make to Be Reflective)	DESIRED OUTCOME
Green Zone SOCIAL EMOTIONAL WELL-BEING			I will use this student's name in greeting. I will recognize a strength she possesses every day. I will ask her about one of her interests outside of school and refer to that interest regularly.	I will acknowledge that I may have made assumptions about this student, and I will create opportunities to get to know her better.	I want my student to care about her studies and engage respectfully in class discussions and activities.

©2021 K. Hamilton Biagas, L. Nathanson, and M. Trujillo

	END STEP 5	STEP 4	STEP 3	STEP 2	START STEP 1
LIFE SITUATION	INTERNAL/ SUBTLE RESPONSES (What this can feel like inside)	EMOTIONS/ FEELINGS (What we experience based on emotions)	EXTERNAL BEHAVIORS (What this can look like)	STRATEGIES (A conscious choice we make to Be Reflective)	DESIRED OUTCOME
Green Zone SOCIAL EMOTIONAL WELL-BEING		Curious Emotionally connected Hopeful	I will use this student's name in greeting. I will recognize a strength she possesses every day. I will ask her about one of her interests outside of school and refer to that interest regularly.	I will acknowledge that I may have made assumptions about this student, and I will create opportunities to get to know her better.	I want my student to care about her studies and engage respectfully in class discussions and activities.

©2021 K. Hamilton Biagas, L. Nathanson, and M. Trujillo

LIFE SITUATION	END STEP 5 — INTERNAL/ SUBTLE RESPONSES (What this can feel like inside)	STEP 4 — EMOTIONS/ FEELINGS (What we experience based on emotions)	STEP 3 — EXTERNAL BEHAVIORS (What this can look like)	STEP 2 — STRATEGIES (A conscious choice we make to Be Reflective)	START STEP 1 — DESIRED OUTCOME
Green Zone SOCIAL EMOTIONAL WELL-BEING	Steady heart rate Calmness Centeredness	Curious Emotionally connected Hopeful	I will use this student's name in greeting. I will recognize a strength she possesses every day. I will ask her about one of her interests outside of school and refer to that interest regularly.	I will acknowledge that I may have made assumptions about this student, and I will create opportunities to get to know her better.	I want my student to care about her studies and engage respectfully in class discussions and activities.

Conscious Connection Challenge: Be Reflective

Now, it is your turn to consider a life situation in which you would like to presume a specific desired outcome. Follow the steps as you fill out the chart from right to left and consider the possibilities. Also, note that you can download a template for the Conscious Connection Challenge here: **www.centerforlearningandwellbeing.com**

Life Situation: _____

	END STEP 5 Ask, "What do I feel in my body?"	STEP 4 Ask, "What am I experiencing or feeling?"	STEP 3 Ask, "What might it look like?"	STEP 2 Ask, "What choice can I make?"	START STEP 1 Ask, "What do I want to make possible?"
LIFE SITUATION	**INTERNAL/ SUBTLE RESPONSES** (What this can feel like inside)	**EMOTIONS/ FEELINGS** (What we experience based on emotions)	**EXTERNAL BEHAVIORS** (What this can look like)	**STRATEGIES** (A conscious choice we make to Be Reflective)	**DESIRED OUTCOME**
Green Zone SOCIAL EMOTIONAL WELL-BEING					

BE REFLECTIVE

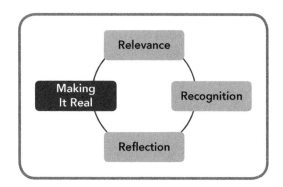

Journaling Opportunity: Feel free to use the space below to write out any thoughts, reminders, "ahas," or curiosities that have occurred to you throughout the *Making It Real* segment.

_____

_____

_____

_____

_____

_____

_____

_____

_____

_____

_____

_____

_____

_____

_____

_____

_____

_____

BE INTENTIONAL

"Close your tabs!" Those of you who read my book *Start With the Heart* (Corwin, 2019) likely remember the story I shared of my husband, David, telling me I needed to close my tabs. Needless to say, I was defensive and offended, though I didn't really know what he meant! Then, he explained that sometimes I remind him of a computer with multiple tabs open. My mind and body are bebopping from one tab to another without ever closing any down—and often, I open more tabs along the way. Without question, I was awestruck by the aptness of his analogy! I realized he was right; I am in go-mode all of the time. I have a great deal of energy, optimism, and enthusiasm, and I have always used these traits to share my passion, connect with others, and, quite simply, to just get things done! At the same time, with David's words in the back of my mind and the middle of my heart, I encountered a few valuable revelations, one of which was the awareness that keeping multiple tabs open leaves no space for intentionality. When I speed from one thought or activity to another, I miss things. In fact, I miss people—often those who are most important to me.

Perhaps this happens to you too. Can you relate to getting caught with all your tabs open? Do you ever feel rushed, overwhelmed, or frenzied? Are there times when you have so much to do that you experience an adrenaline rush, as your concentration wanders and your frustration explodes? Or perhaps you find yourself functioning on autopilot, walking right by someone, asking "How are you?" and never stopping to acknowledge their response. Conversely, maybe you find yourself on the opposite side of the spectrum, stuck in complacency or apathy. Do any of these situations sound familiar to you? If the answer is even a small degree of yes, then your social emotional well-being may benefit from increasing your awareness and practice of being intentional.

Needless to say, when we fail to be intentional, we inadvertently neglect our social emotional well-being, and it can have a negative impact on our social, mental, physical, and spiritual health. Being intentional, on the other hand, helps us to find balance and peace, even in the midst of our busy lives (or in my case, in the midst of my tendency toward hyperactivity). Not that balance comes naturally to all of us, but when we do focus on being intentional, it makes a difference in how we feel in our bodies, in our appreciation of the little things (because we actually notice them!), and in the quality of our relationships. Let's jump into *Relevance* to discover what it might look like to Be Intentional.

BE INTENTIONAL

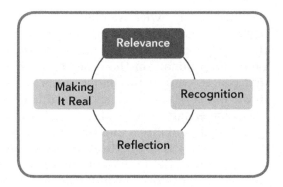

WHAT does it mean and look like to Be Intentional?

Being intentional means thinking, speaking, and behaving with purpose. The primary focus includes, but is not limited to these actions:

- Noticing the physical manifestations of our emotions or feelings
- Being mindful of our attitudes, words, and behaviors
- Taking intentional breaths to center, focus, or reset
- Focusing on that which is within our realm of control
- Having a growth mindset focused on strengths and possibilities
- Practicing stress and time management techniques
- Connecting with others purposely
- Listening actively, with our whole mind and body

WHY is it relevant to social emotional well-being?

- *Personal Relevance*: Being intentional contributes to mindfulness and presence. Intentionality helps us to slow down, breathe, and prioritize our social, emotional, physical, and spiritual health.
- *Professional Relevance*: Our vocations as educators can be stressful. With intention, we can set realistic goals, as well as boundaries. Intentionality also cultivates authenticity, which can help us to build relationships with our students, their families, and our colleagues.

SEL Connection: Self-Management

BE INTENTIONAL

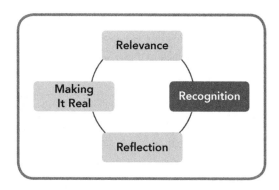

Relevance

Making It Real

Recognition

Reflection

It is time again to recognize strengths you possess that can be leveraged to nourish your social emotional well-being. Take a moment to highlight one or two statements that stand out to you as personal or vocational strengths. As I suggested previously, feel free to add a strength or two not listed at the bottom of the list.

BE INTENTIONAL
I focus on one task at a time.
I set aside my phone when in the presence of others.
I remember people's names when first introduced.
I am organized and take time to practice stress management techniques.
I let go of situations that are out of my control.
I give myself grace when my plans don't go as I intended.
I leave work *at* work in order to focus on family, friends, and/or personal responsibilities at home.
I allow myself to try new things, even if failure is likely, in order to learn and grow.
I redirect or walk away from negative conversations.
If I see an unjust situation occur, I say something or do something in an effort to promote justice.
I structure each day so that when my students walk into my class, I can immediately give them my full attention.
When I feel anxious, frustrated, angry, overexcited, or any other emotion that causes my adrenaline to increase, I take at least one intentional breath.
When I feel overwhelmed or frustrated, I calmly let others know how I am feeling and/or request a moment to breathe or refocus.

Considering the row or two that you highlighted, or a strength you may have added, what does the practice of this way of being look like in your life?

_____

_____

_____

_____

How might the practice of your highlighted strength or strengths positively impact your well-being?

_____

_____

_____

How might the practice of your highlighted strength or strengths positively impact those with whom you interact, care for, or love?

_____

_____

_____

_____

How might you leverage at least one of these strengths in order to provide an opportunity for another to feel valued or appreciated?

_____

_____

_____

_____

Let me remind you that you may find it helpful, as we continue our journey through each way of being, to revisit your strengths and to ask yourself how you might reframe a challenge or opportunity for growth by leveraging your strengths. Speaking of revisiting, are you ready to step into the *Reflection* segment of being intentional?

BE INTENTIONAL

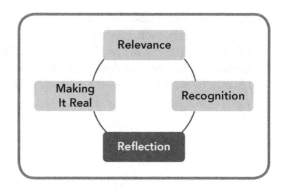

Irony greets us again as we lean into reflecting upon our efforts to be intentional, as reflection in and of itself takes intentionality. I believe you will begin to see why I created the framework as a circular puzzle in which every piece, or way of being, is interconnected. Every individual way of being relies upon and enhances the others. Specifically, in regard to being intentional, the effective use of the Framework for Social Emotional Well-Being requires that we *be* intentional. For without intentionality, our conviction to nourish our social emotional well-being will be lacking. Intentionality, however, breeds purpose and significance. John C. Maxwell, known for his best-selling books, pastoral wisdom, and practical ideas, suggests, "Being intentional adds value to everything we do and every person we meet."[2]

So the pertinent question is this: Does the way in which you live your life include being intentional? And if so, to what degree? If you haven't *intentionally* reflected upon your endeavor to be intentional, let's do so now, using the Tiered Continuum of Questions.

---

[2]John C. Maxwell, *Intentional Living: Choosing a Life That Matters* (New York: Center Street, 2017).

Tier 1: Universal Practices
We can ALL ask these questions:

- Do I understand the definition of self-management?
- When I notice my emotions are physically manifested in my body language or body response, what helps me to recenter or refocus in order to use my emotions in a way that is helpful to the situation?
- Have I identified at least two stress management strategies that help me to feel calm or more focused?
- Do I ask myself, "What is within my realm of control?" and then set achievable goals based on the answer?
- Do I let go of those things out of my realm of control? If so, what does that look like for me? If not, what does *that* look like? Either way, does the result help or hinder my way of being or my relationships with others?
- Do I take initiative to stand up for myself, personally and/or professionally, even when it may be uncomfortable? What does it look like when I do this?
- Am I intentional in my interactions and communication with others? Do I make purposeful connections and actively listen to others?
- Do I intentionally seek guidance on how to discuss race and understand events and experiences through the lens of race, culture, and power in a way that normalizes the content and conversation, without causing harm?

Tier 2: Targeted Supports and/or Interventions
SOME of us may benefit from following up with these questions:

- Would it help to talk to another person or people I trust in order to get an objective perspective of how my emotions show up in my body response or language?
- Would I benefit from small-group support or a class to learn more about these items?
  - Stress management strategies
  - Time management strategies
  - Goal-setting strategies
  - Anger management strategies
  - Mindfulness strategies
  - Equity-based communication strategies
  - o If so, what resources are available to seek support or learning opportunities?
- Do I have a desire to take initiative in standing up for myself or others, but I'm not comfortable, nor do I feel able to do so?
  - o If so, is there another person I trust who has a strength in this area from whom I can seek guidance?

  OR

  - o Are there community resources available with services that might help me to develop my ability to take initiative?

Tier 3: Intensive Individualized Supports and/or Interventions
A FEW of us may ask ourselves these questions:

- Does my response to my feelings tend to manifest in a physical response that feels or appears detrimental to my mental, emotional, or physical health?
- Does the way in which I express my emotions or manage my time negatively impact my health or my relationships?
- If I answered YES to either of these questions, might it help to seek the support of a counselor, psychologist, or psychiatrist to learn mindfulness or self-regulation strategies specific to my needs?

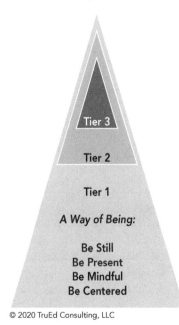

Tier 3

Tier 2

Tier 1

A Way of Being:

Be Still
Be Present
Be Mindful
Be Centered

© 2020 TruEd Consulting, LLC

Be Intentional
Tiered Continuum
Questions

BE INTENTIONAL

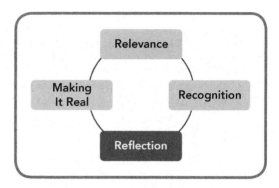

In consideration of how you might challenge yourself in this way of being, please use the following question prompts to reflect upon your practice of being intentional.

What do I notice about myself?

_____

_____

_____

_____

Were there any questions that were difficult for me to answer? If so, why?

_____

_____

_____

_____

Did my answers surprise me in any way? If so, why?

_____

_____

_____

_____

Is there anything else that occurs to me as I reflect upon what *being intentional* looks like, feels like, or means in my life?

_____

_____

_____

_____

Again, I have chosen a question for you to use as an example in the Guided Reflection Flowchart, a template to choose your own question, and a blank page to create your own flow.

Guided Reflection Flowchart Template

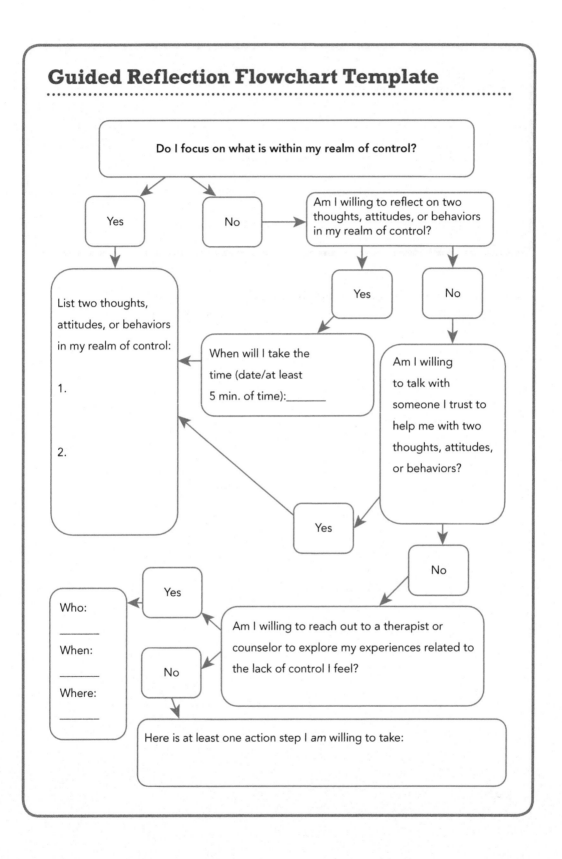

Do I focus on what is within my realm of control?

Yes

No

Am I willing to reflect on two thoughts, attitudes, or behaviors in my realm of control?

Yes

No

List two thoughts, attitudes, or behaviors in my realm of control:

1.

2.

When will I take the time (date/at least 5 min. of time):_____

Am I willing to talk with someone I trust to help me with two thoughts, attitudes, or behaviors?

Yes

No

Yes

Who:
_____
When:
_____
Where:
_____

Am I willing to reach out to a therapist or counselor to explore my experiences related to the lack of control I feel?

No

Here is at least one action step I *am* willing to take:

Reflection Flowchart Template

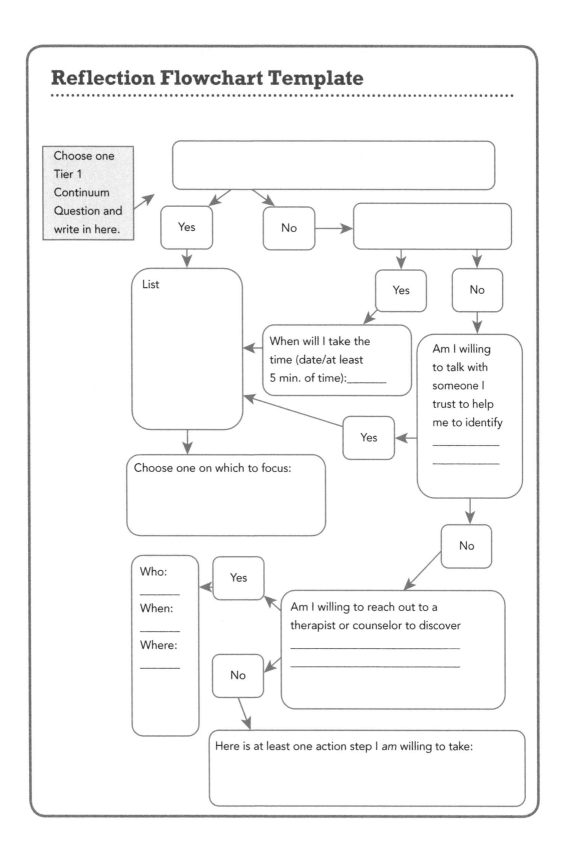

Choose one Tier 1 Continuum Question and write in here.

Yes

No

List

Yes

No

When will I take the time (date/at least 5 min. of time):_____

Am I willing to talk with someone I trust to help me to identify

_____
_____

Yes

Choose one on which to focus:

No

Who:
_____
When:
_____
Where:
_____

Yes

No

Am I willing to reach out to a therapist or counselor to discover

_____
_____

Here is at least one action step I *am* willing to take:

Reflection Flowchart: Create Your Own

BE INTENTIONAL

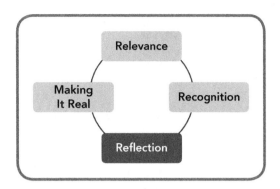

Journaling Opportunity: Feel free to use the space below to write out any thoughts, reminders, "ahas," or curiosities that have occurred to you throughout the *Reflection* segment.

_____

_____

_____

_____

_____

_____

_____

_____

_____

_____

_____

_____

_____

_____

BE INTENTIONAL

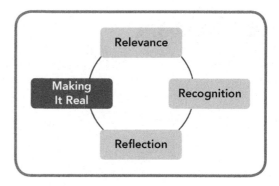

Thank you for taking time to engage in reflection. Now, let's apply being intentional to our Cultivation Challenge and Conscious Connection Challenge.

Cultivation Challenge: Making It Real in Three, Two, One!

Three: Answer these three questions. (*Note*: Change "I" to "we" if accepting this challenge as a group.)

1. What is one area in which I have an opportunity for growth regarding my awareness or practice of being intentional?

_____

_____

2. Why did I choose this area for growth?

_____

_____

_____

_____

3. If I were to grow or improve in this area, what would it make possible in my personal and/ or professional life?

_____

_____

_____

_____

Two: List at least two ideas or ways that I might cultivate my opportunity for growth.

1. _____

_____

_____

2. _____

_____

_____

One: Choose one idea to apply. Use the Growth Action Plan table to record one idea, practice, and track and then celebrate or revise that idea or way to cultivate growth.

1. Growth Action Plan

OPPORTUNITY FOR GROWTH	PRACTICE	TRACK	CELEBRATE OR REVISE
List one idea or way to cultivate growth.	List one internal (thought/attitude) and one external (words, behaviors) element to practice.	Set a tangible goal for the week and tally the times per day you engage in practice.	Record a star or checkmark at the end of the week if your goal is met or revise your goal to scaffold your practice if necessary.
1.	1.	Goal:	Celebrate:
	2.	Tally:	Revise:

Conscious Connection Challenge: Be Intentional

Life Situation: _____

Conscious Connection Challenge: Follow the steps as you fill out the chart from right to left and consider the possibilities.

Step 1: Based on a specific life situation, determine a desired outcome you would like to achieve in your personal or professional life.

Step 2: Define one conscious choice you *could* make in the realm of a specific way of *being intentional* in order to achieve your desired outcome.

Step 3: Explain what it might look like if the outcome were to be achieved.

Step 4: List two to three emotions or feeling words that may be experienced if the outcome were to be achieved.

Step 5: List one or two internal or subtle responses that may be present if the outcome were to be achieved.

	END STEP 5 ←	STEP 4 ←	STEP 3 ←	STEP 2 ←	START STEP 1 ←
LIFE SITUATION	**INTERNAL/ SUBTLE RESPONSES** (What this feels like inside)	**EMOTIONS/ FEELINGS** (What we experience based on emotions)	**EXTERNAL BEHAVIORS** (What this looks like)	**STRATEGIES** (A conscious choice we make to Be Intentional)	**DESIRED OUTCOME**
Green Zone SOCIAL EMOTIONAL WELL-BEING					

BE INTENTIONAL

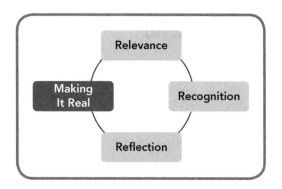

Journaling Opportunity: Feel free to use the space below to write out any thoughts, reminders, "ahas," or curiosities that have occurred to you throughout the *Making It Real* segment.

_____

_____

_____

_____

_____

_____

_____

_____

_____

_____

_____

_____

_____

_____

_____

_____

_____

_____

BE EMPATHETIC

Henry David Thoreau wrote, "Could a greater miracle take place than for us to look through each other's eyes for an instant?"[3] I wonder at the potential that lies within this question. Yes, it would be *the* miracle of utmost proportions if all humans on Earth could, in fact, look through each other's eyes. So as we step into our third way of being, to Be Empathetic, I ask that we consider the possibilities that being empathetic might create in our lives and the lives of those with whom we interact. First, however, it is helpful to understand that there is a difference between empathy and sympathy. Sympathy is a genuine sadness for what someone else may be going through, and though it may be sincere, it rarely is helpful because it often relies on words rather than action. Empathy, however, is active compassion. Empathy steps into the moment *with* someone as they experience hardship, grief, or challenging life experiences.

To be empathetic requires that we are not only aware, or sensitive to, another person's feelings or situation, but that we authentically seek to understand what they are experiencing. This doesn't mean that we *will* understand, nor is actually understanding a requirement of empathy. In fact, my former students have suggested that they felt most supported when I said to them, "I have absolutely no idea what you are going through. But I am here. I am with you, and I want to understand. Can you tell me more?" It is the wanting, the seeking to understand that matters. This is where compassion, kindness, curiosity, and respect live. There is no place for judgment and no need for advice. Often, empathy is quiet and still. It looks like listening and feels like comfort.

---

[3]Henry David Thoreau, *Walden, or Life in the Woods* (New York: New American Library, 1954), 13. (Original work published 1919.)

Furthermore, to be empathetic is to be more socially aware. Because empathy seeks to understand, it inspires us to learn about race, ethnicity, gender, ability, religion, and socioeconomic status, especially when those characteristics differ from our own. Empathy encourages courageous vulnerability and sincere curiosity. Sometimes, it is uncomfortable to talk about issues such racism or gender identity, yet how will we learn and grow if we don't step into discomfort? Even dipping our toe in by asking open-ended questions, engaging in curious conversations, or reading or listening to music outside our norms will lead to greater understanding and enhanced social awareness. Contributing to the needs of one's community also breeds empathy because service to others helps us to see outside ourselves.

Finally, being empathetic is vital to our social emotional well-being and that of all humans because it is through empathy that human connection flourishes. Let me put it in vocational context. Classroom teachers often get frustrated by the behavior of students in their classroom or overwhelmed by the need to improve test scores. When this happens, the focus becomes behavior or assessment data. Not that using data isn't important—the administrator in me knows that using data to make decisions is essential to guide decision-making in the realm of behavior or achievement. Yet sometimes we get so ultrafocused on correcting behavior or teaching to a standardized test that we lose sight of "who" we are correcting or teaching. Empathy reminds us that there is a child behind every piece of data and a human being behind every behavior. When we shift our focus to the human element of our work, we will stay more connected to our purpose and nurture stronger relationships with our students and colleagues. In doing so, we also nurture our own well-being.

BE EMPATHETIC

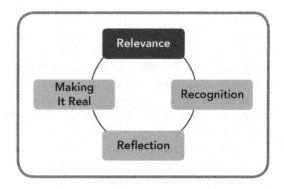

WHAT does it mean and look like to Be Empathetic?

Being empathetic means seeking to understand. The primary focus includes, but is not limited to these actions:

- Demonstrating active compassion

- Approaching people and situations with an open mind and an open heart

- Being with others, even when we don't understand

- Listening first, talking less

- Practicing courageous vulnerability

- Appreciating and honoring differences among peoples and cultures

WHY is it relevant to social emotional well-being?

- *Personal Relevance*: Being empathetic can nurture selflessness, kindness, and understanding. These acts suppress negativity, judgment, and angst, which in turn helps us to have a more positive attitude and peaceful spirit.

- *Professional Relevance*: Empathy helps us remember that there are stories behind the behaviors of our students (and our colleagues). When we focus on correcting behavior rather than judging the person, we will nurture stronger relationships, better classroom management, and more authentic communication.

SEL Connection: Social Awareness

BE EMPATHETIC

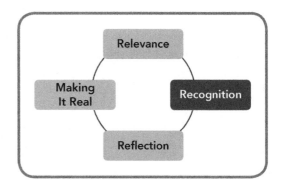

When you consider what being empathetic looks like in your life, do you recognize strengths in your thoughts, attitudes, and behaviors? Please review the statements from our Social Emotional Well-Being Check-In, then highlight at least two strengths or add your own to the bottom of the check-in.

BE EMPATHETIC
I listen well without thinking about what I want to say in response.
I listen without interrupting, even when I disagree with what is being shared.
In unfamiliar situations, I seek *first* to understand.
I refrain from making judgments about others whose lives and experience may be different from mine.
I am compassionate when someone is in need.
I take the perspective of others in order to attempt to see situations, ideas, and opinions through their viewpoint.
I read articles and books that inform my understanding of disparities that exist regarding race, ethnicity, gender, ability, religion, and socioeconomic status, especially those that differ from my own.
I initiate conversations with people who have life experiences that differ from mine in an effort to gain insight and understanding.
I engage in restorative practices in an effort to build relationships with others.
I ask "What happened?" or "Can you tell me more?" as opposed to "Why did you do that?"
I participate in opportunities to serve my community.

Considering the row or two that you highlighted, or a strength you may have added, what does the practice of this way of being look like in your life?

_____

_____

_____

_____

How might the practice of your highlighted strength or strengths positively impact your well-being?

_____

_____

_____

_____

How might the practice of your highlighted strength or strengths positively impact those with whom you interact, care for, or love?

_____

_____

_____

_____

How might you leverage at least one of these strengths in order to provide an opportunity for another to feel valued or appreciated?

_____

_____

_____

_____

I hope that you have found it enlightening to recognize your strengths and to think through how these strengths benefit your own well-being and that of those with whom you interact. As with all ways of being, in addition to strengths, we all have opportunities to cultivate growth. The questions found in the Be Empathetic Tiered Continuum may help you reflect upon areas in your personal or professional life that you can cultivate to become more empathetic.

BE EMPATHETIC

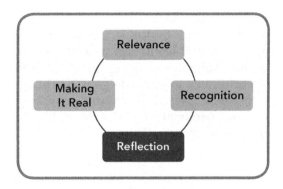

As we reflect upon what it means to cultivate empathy, I want to ask you to think back over some of the challenges that you or your loved ones faced during the height of the pandemic. During that time, I often heard people refer to COVID-19 as the great equalizer. People expressed and some drew comfort from the idea that we, as humans upon this earth, were all experiencing the same perilous situation. Though there is truth in that statement, it is also true that people experienced the pandemic differently. African American communities and the elderly were at a much higher risk of losing their lives to the disease. Some families had limited access to food, household supplies, medication, and education. Others had the capacity to purchase groceries and necessary provisions online. Privilege, poverty, instability, affluence, inaccessibility, abundance, or just enough—what was your experience? Acknowledging that yours may have been different than someone else's is the first step in cultivating an empathetic way of being.

Once we acknowledge that everyone has their own story, we will begin to notice disparities and disproportionalities requiring attention and reform. We might also identify commonalities. Continuing to use the pandemic as an example, I think we can acknowledge that we all experienced loss—admittedly, to different degrees. Most of us lost the freedom to move about without thought or fear for our safety or that of our loved ones. Some of us experienced the loss of family income, while others experienced the loss of health. Ultimately, more people than we can count are still grieving the loss of loved ones. You might be counted among them. Those of us who have encountered the grief journey know that it can breed an unsolicited gift in providing us with the empirical ability to be empathetic. Not only are we able to be *with* others in their grief, but we also truly understand that one doesn't get "over" grief or get "through" it. For people who have never experienced the loss of a loved one, the need to be empathetic is paramount because when a person is grieving, their words or behaviors may not match what they are thinking or feeling on the inside. In this situation, to be empathetic is to be patient, accepting, and kind while our students, colleagues, or friends experience their grief, in their own time and in their own way.

I admit that I have given you a great deal to think about. For that reason, as you consider the Tiered Continuum questions, please remember that the universal Tier 1 practices of being open-minded, curious, compassionate, and respectful are key to being empathetic. Also recall that universal ways of being are constant throughout the continuum. So as you reflect on the questions at each level of the continuum, please apply being open-minded, curious, compassionate, and respectful toward yourself, realizing that it is much easier for some of us to bestow these qualities on others than it is to relate them to ourselves.

Be Empathetic Tiered Continuum Questions

Tier 3

Tier 2

Tier 1
A Way of Being:

**Be Open-Minded
Be Curious
Be Compassionate
Be Respectful**

© 2020 TruEd Consulting, LLC

Tier 1: Universal Practices
We can ALL ask these questions:

- Do I understand the definition of social awareness?
- Do I understand the difference between empathy and sympathy?
- Do I value and practice recognizing strengths in others and taking others' perspective?
- Do I show compassion and empathy for others? What might that look like for me?
- Do I seek opportunities to listen?
- Do I look for opportunities to say, "Tell me more . . ."?
- Do I seek to understand the stories or situations behind the behaviors or ways of being of another?
- Do I pursue opportunities to learn about race, ethnicity, gender, ability, religion, and socioeconomic status, especially those that differ from my own?
- Do I practice being restorative by using affective statements and asking affective questions?
- Do I understand the Social Discipline Window?

Tier 2: Targeted Supports and/or Interventions
SOME of us may benefit from following up with these questions:

- Do I find myself making assumptions about a specific person or groups of people?
  - Do I have a trusted friend or colleague with whom I can discuss the potential consequences or impact of my assumptions?
- Would I benefit from a workshop, course, or training to learn more about these issues?
  - Empathy training
  - Social and/or racial justice awareness
  - Gender identity
  - Relationship-centered learning
  - Proactive restorative practices
  - Trauma-informed care
  - _____ (Other)
- Do my implicit biases show up explicitly, and might a workshop, training, or course help me to be more socially aware?

Tier 3: Intensive Individualized Supports and/or Interventions
A FEW of us may ask ourselves these questions:

- Does my lack of social awareness have negative implications for me or others?
- Do I notice that I tend to hurt or offend people with my words or behaviors? Even unintentionally?
- Have I ever been told by a trusted friend or colleague that I am narcissistic? Have I reflected on that information with genuine curiosity and a desire to see another's views or perspectives?
- If I answered YES to any of these questions, might it help to seek the support of a counselor, psychologist, or psychiatrist to guide me in becoming more empathetic?

BE EMPATHETIC

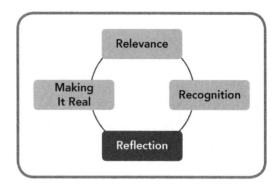

Please use the following question prompts to reflect upon how you live out being empathetic and areas in which you might grow or improve this way of being in your life.

What do I notice about myself?

_____

_____

_____

_____

Were there any questions that were difficult for me to answer? If so, why?

_____

_____

_____

_____

Did my answers surprise me in any way? If so, why?

_____

_____

_____

_____

(Continued)

(Continued)

Is there anything else that occurs to me as I reflect upon what *being empathetic* looks like, feels like, or means in my life?

_____

_____

_____

_____

Feel free to use the following templates to help you to process your reflections.

Guided Reflection Flowchart Template

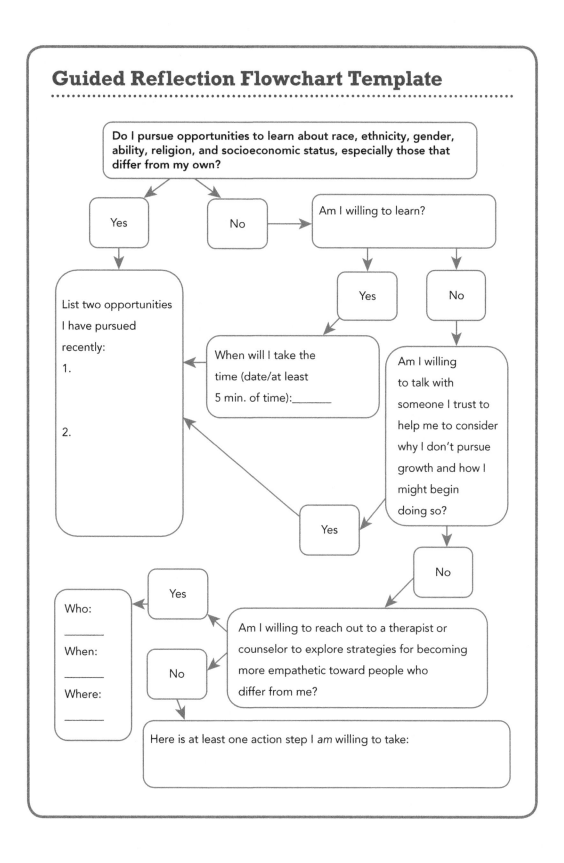

Do I pursue opportunities to learn about race, ethnicity, gender, ability, religion, and socioeconomic status, especially those that differ from my own?

Yes

No

Am I willing to learn?

Yes

No

List two opportunities I have pursued recently:

1.

2.

When will I take the time (date/at least 5 min. of time):_____

Am I willing to talk with someone I trust to help me to consider why I don't pursue growth and how I might begin doing so?

Yes

No

Who:
_____
When:
_____
Where:
_____

Yes

No

Am I willing to reach out to a therapist or counselor to explore strategies for becoming more empathetic toward people who differ from me?

Here is at least one action step I *am* willing to take:

Reflection Flowchart Template

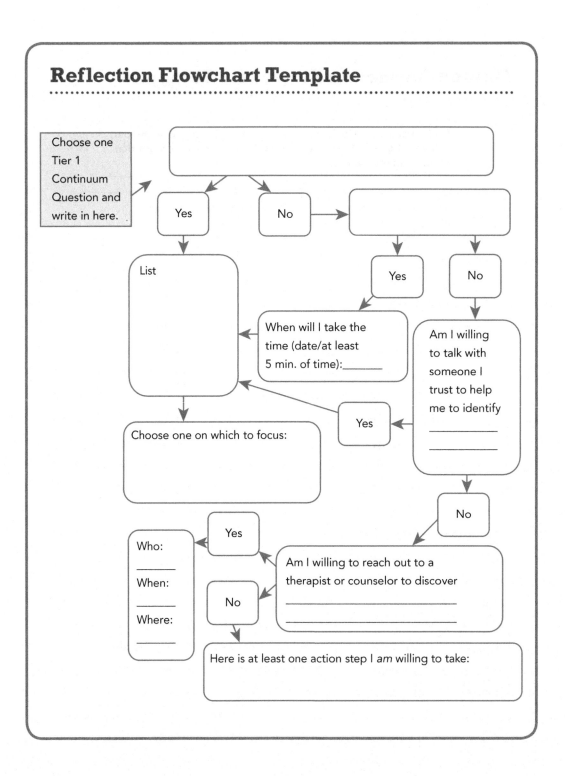

Choose one Tier 1 Continuum Question and write in here.

Yes

No

List

Yes

No

When will I take the time (date/at least 5 min. of time):_____

Am I willing to talk with someone I trust to help me to identify _____ _____

Yes

Choose one on which to focus:

No

Yes

Who: _____

When: _____

Where: _____

No

Am I willing to reach out to a therapist or counselor to discover _____ _____

Here is at least one action step I *am* willing to take:

Reflection Flowchart: Create Your Own

BE EMPATHETIC

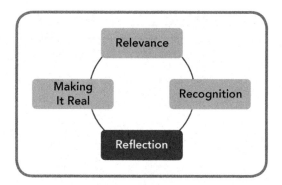

Journaling Opportunity: Feel free to use the space below to write out any thoughts, reminders, "ahas," or curiosities that have occurred to you throughout the *Reflection* segment.

_____

_____

_____

_____

_____

_____

_____

_____

_____

_____

_____

_____

_____

_____

_____

_____

_____

BE EMPATHETIC

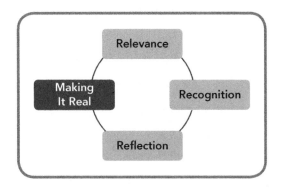

Take a moment to take one intentional breath before you engage in the Cultivation Challenge and Conscious Connection Challenge. You just spent time reflecting upon your way of being empathetic. As you breathe in slowly through your nose, please bring into your mind a picture of what empathy looks like, hold that picture for a second or two in your mind and heart, and then, as you slowly blow your breath out through your mouth, visualize this picture permeating its way into the world.

Now, let's switch gears and focus on a specific way in which to develop our awareness or practice of being empathetic through our Cultivation Challenge.

Cultivation Challenge: Making It Real in Three, Two, One!

Three: Answer these three questions. (*Note:* Change "I" to "we" if accepting this challenge as a group.)

1. What is one area in which I have an opportunity for growth regarding my awareness or practice of being empathetic?

_____

_____

2. Why did I choose this area for growth?

_____

_____

(Continued)

(Continued)

_____

_____

3. If I were to grow or improve in this area, what would it make possible in my personal and/or professional life?

_____

_____

_____

_____

Two: List at least two ideas or ways that I might cultivate my opportunity for growth.

1. _____

_____

_____

2. _____

_____

_____

One: Choose one idea to apply. Use the Growth Action Plan table to record one idea, practice, and track and then celebrate or revise that idea or way to cultivate growth.

1. Growth Action Plan

OPPORTUNITY FOR GROWTH	PRACTICE	TRACK	CELEBRATE OR REVISE
List one idea or way to cultivate growth.	List one internal (thought/attitude) and one external (words, behaviors) element to practice.	Set a tangible goal for the week and tally the times per day you engage in practice.	Record a star or checkmark at the end of the week if your goal is met or revise your goal to scaffold your practice if necessary.

OPPORTUNITY FOR GROWTH	PRACTICE	TRACK	CELEBRATE OR REVISE
1.	1.	Goal:	Celebrate:
	2.	Tally:	Revise:

Remember that tracking, celebrating, and/or revising is vital to our personal or professional growth. I realize it takes intentional effort and even a bit of time, but in the long run, it will provide you with information to celebrate, improve, and, ultimately, nourish your social emotional well-being. The Conscious Connection Challenge will do the same. Thank you for exploring a life situation related to being empathetic for which you can reverse engineer a desired outcome.

Conscious Connection Challenge: Be Empathetic

Step 1: Determine a desired outcome you would like to achieve in your personal or professional life.

Step 2: Define one conscious choice you *could* make in the realm of a specific way of being **empathetic** in order to achieve your desired outcome.

Step 3: Explain what it might look like if the outcome were to be achieved.

Step 4: List two to three emotions or feeling words that may be experienced if outcome were to be achieved.

Step 5: List one or two internal or subtle responses that may be present if the outcome were to be achieved.

(Continued)

(Continued)

Conscious Connection Challenge: Follow the steps as you fill out the chart from right to left and consider the possibilities.

Life Situation: _____

LIFE SITUATION	END STEP 5 ← INTERNAL/ SUBTLE RESPONSES (What this feels like inside)	STEP 4 ← EMOTIONS/ FEELINGS (What we experience based on emotions)	STEP 3 ← EXTERNAL BEHAVIORS (What this looks like)	STEP 2 ← STRATEGIES (A conscious choice we make to Be Empathetic)	START STEP 1 ← DESIRED OUTCOME
Green Zone SOCIAL EMOTIONAL WELL-BEING					

©2021 K. Hamilton Biagas, L. Nathanson, and M. Trujillo

BE EMPATHETIC

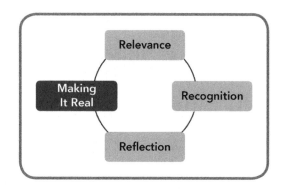

Relevance

Making It Real

Recognition

Reflection

Journaling Opportunity: Feel free to use the space below to write out any thoughts, reminders, "ahas," or curiosities that have occurred to you throughout the *Making It Real* segment.

_____

_____

_____

_____

_____

_____

_____

_____

_____

_____

_____

_____

_____

_____

_____

_____

_____

_____

_____

_____

_____

BE CONNECTED

It is not a coincidence that the Be Connected puzzle piece inter-links with the Be Empathetic piece in the Framework for Social Emotional Well-Being. Remember, when we *be* empathetic, human connection thrives. If the COVID-19 pandemic taught us nothing else, it certainly reminded us of the value of human connection. Many of us spent much of the spring of 2020 and months there-after in isolation—disconnected from extended family members, friends, colleagues, and students. Some of us experienced loneli-ness, lethargy, or depression as a result. If you reflect and count yourself in this group, know that you are not alone. Connection is fundamental to our social emotional well-being.

To be connected is to be invested in a relationship and engaged with others. Though some of us may value our independence and appreciate time in solitude (this is actually a very important self-care practice for some of us), we also need social interac-tion. Research demonstrates that when we make positive social interactions we actually "feel" better. According to research fel-low Valentina Colonnello and her colleagues, a review of various prominent studies has revealed that "positive social interactions may have protective effects for health, both directly, through their regulatory role in an individual's physiological functions, and indirectly, through their buffering of responses to stressful life experiences."[4] For example, when we have a social interaction that is positive in nature, there is a release of neurotransmitters in our brain (dopamine, serotonin, and oxytocin) that cause feelings of happiness, while the chemical that induces a stress response (cortisol) is diminished.

---

[4] Valentina Colonnello, Nicola Petrocchi, Marina Farinelli, and Cristina Ottaviani, "Positive Social Interactions in a Lifespan Perspective With a Focus on Opioidergic and Oxytocinergic Systems: Implications for Neuroprotection," *Current Neuropharmacology* 15, no. 4 (2017): 543–61.

We also learned during the pandemic that social and emotion connection is paramount, especially when physical contact is unsafe. As an educator, I have always promoted kinesthetic connection. I know from experience that connecting with kids as they enter the classroom by way of a handshake, high five, or fist bump can make a marked difference in attitude and classroom behavior. Yet when close physical contact was determined to spread disease, we discovered other ways to be connected socially and emotionally.

Using a person's name in greeting and making eye contact (when appropriate) are two ways to be connected. Both say, "I see you," which we know is relevant to students being interested and engaged in school. Smiling authentically, so that the joy that lives in our hearts is expressed through our eyes, will also foster emotional connection and nourish our own well-being as well as that of those with whom we connect.

Being connected grows relationships because it fosters trust, compassion, and collaboration. It says, "I'm here, I care, and we are in this together!" Together, let's explore the *Relevance*, *Recognition*, *Reflection*, and *Making It Real* segments of being connected.

BE CONNECTED

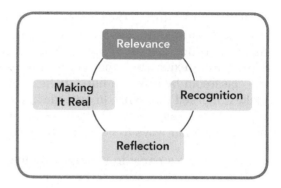

WHAT does it mean and look like to Be Connected?

Being connected means relating to others emotionally, socially, kinesthetically, and spiritually. Primary focus includes, but is not limited to these actions:

- Seeking to develop and sustain healthy relationships
- Asking "How are you?" and listening to the answer
- Smiling authentically
- Communicating with clarity and compassion
- Collaborating with others to find solutions
- Pursuing opportunities to humbly support humanity
- Asking for help

WHY is it relevant to social emotional well-being?

- *Personal Relevance*: Connection neutralizes isolation, which is vital because the lack of human connection can lead to loneliness, anxiety, or depression. Being connected, therefore, can grow relationships, increase feelings of belonging, improve our self-worth and confidence, and ultimately boost our immune system.

- *Professional Relevance*: Being connected can inspire empathy, grow student/educator or collegial relationships, and foster a positive sense of self. Intentional connection can cultivate positive school culture and climate and can improve job satisfaction, helping us to experience less work-related overwhelm or stress.

SEL Connection: Relationship Skills

BE CONNECTED

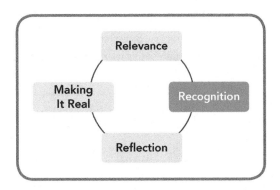

What strengths do you possess when it comes to being connected? Consider the statements from our Social Emotional Well-Being Check-In. Highlight at least two strengths or add your own in the open spaces.

BE CONNECTED
I make eye contact with others (if/when appropriate) and greet people by name.
I kinesthetically connect with others when safe and appropriate (i.e., handshake, high five, fist bump, or side hug).
I ask, "How are you?" and stop to look at the person as I listen to their answer.
I seek to understand the story behind the customs, traditions, and ways of being of others.
I establish healthy relationships that enrich my social emotional well-being.
I maintain healthy relationships that enrich my social emotional well-being.
I communicate well with others.
I willingly collaborate and work well with others.
I practice random acts of kindness.
I offer assistance without hesitation when a student, colleague, or friend needs support or help.
I offer assistance without hesitation when a stranger with whom I cross paths needs support or help.
I share my vocational passion, talents, and interests with others.
I demonstrate respect for others by listening well and honoring their views and perspectives.
I take time to get to know others by showing interest in their endeavors and asking them to share their life or learning experiences.

Considering the row or two that you highlighted, or a strength you may have added, what does the practice of this way of being look like in your life?

_____

_____

_____

_____

How might the practice of your highlighted strength or strengths positively impact your well-being?

_____

_____

_____

_____

How might the practice of your highlighted strength or strengths positively impact those with whom you interact, care for, or love?

_____

_____

_____

_____

How might you leverage at least one of these strengths in order to provide an opportunity for another to feel valued or appreciated?

_____

_____

_____

_____

Thank you again for taking time to recognize your strengths. Leveraging our strengths in regard to being connected will undoubtedly enhance our personal and vocational relationships. Educators never hesitate to recognize the value of association between building relationships and academic engagement. In fact, if you think back to teachers or school staff members from your past who had an impact on your life, what qualities or assets come to mind? I would presume that the virtues you thought of had more to do with the way in which they connected with you, than it did with their mastery of subject matter. Take a moment to write some of those qualities here:

_____

_____

_____

_____

_____

_____

_____

As we begin the *Reflection* section, be aware of the virtues you associated with in an impactful teacher and consider if you possess or can cultivate those qualities yourself.

BE CONNECTED

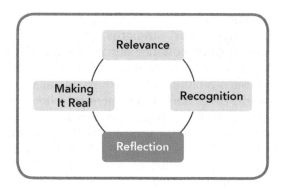

There are many opportunities to grow that can be found in the way in which we connect with others. Consider the universal connected ways of being: Be communicative, trustworthy, and appreciative. Look for overlaps in the ways of being we have already discussed. Think about it. Being intentional with our words and body language helps us to better communicate. Being empathetic establishes trustworthiness, and being reflective promotes an awareness of that for which we are grateful. Thus, being reflective, intentional, and empathetic influence one's capacity to be connected and to establish and sustain strong relationships.

As you contemplate the questions within the Tiered Continuum, consider choosing communication, trustworthiness, or gratitude as a lens through which to focus so as to expand your personal or vocational identity. In doing so, you may connect with significance to values that foster your well-being, as you seek to connect more authentically with others.

Tier 1: Universal Practices
We can ALL ask these questions:

- Do I understand the definition of relationship skills?
- Do I understand the difference between emotional, social, and kinesthetic connection?
- Do I greet people by name and use eye contact when appropriate?
- Am I able to establish and maintain healthy relationships?
- Do I communicate with others in a way that is positive and productive?
- Do I collaborate well with others and contribute in a way that fosters teamwork?
- Do I intentionally listen with the purpose of understanding and valuing the strengths and experiences of others?
    - If so, does this include colleagues, students, and their families?
- Do I attempt to connect with others by using names, showing interest in their pursuits, and building trust?
- Am I willing to consider areas in which I would benefit from growth? If so, am I willing to evaluate potential areas in which I demonstrate implicit bias?

Tier 2: Targeted Supports and/or Interventions
SOME of us may benefit from following up with these questions:

- Do I have difficulty developing relationships, working in groups, or collaborating with others?
    - If so, am I willing to learn more about relational skills or collaboration and practice with a trusted friend or colleague?
    - Am I willing to look at areas in need of growth or improvement in my own words or behaviors?
- Do I struggle to communicate my ideas clearly, or do I avoid communication because I often feel misunderstood?
- Would I benefit from small-group support or workshops to learn more about the following topics?
    - Relationship-building strategies
    - Collaboration or teamwork
    - Active listening
    - Equity through the lens of race, culture, or privelege
    - Effective communication strategies
    - Restorative practice awareness
- Would I benefit from participating in a guided restorative conversation with someone with whom I have conflict?
    - If so, is there a trained colleague or supervisor on staff with whom I can initiate this process?

Be Connected Tiered Continuum Questions

Tier 3

Tier 2

Tier 1
A Way of Being:

Be Kind
Be Communicative
Be Trustworthy
Be Appreciative

© 2020 TruEd Consulting, LLC

Tier 3: Intensive Individualized Supports and/or Interventions
A FEW of us may ask ourselves these questions:

- Do I avoid interacting with others or working on a team?
- Do I tend to break trust repeatedly?
- Do I act in a way that is perceived to be disrespectful, even if I don't realize it at the time?
- Do my relationships tend to be consistently destructive or unhealthy?
- If I answered YES to any of these questions, might I benefit from seeking the support of a counselor, psychologist, or psychiatrist to support my desire or efforts to improve my relational skills?

BE CONNECTED

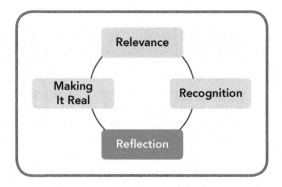

Please use the following question prompts to reflect upon how you live out being connected and areas in which you might grow or improve this way of being in your life.

What do I notice about myself?

_____

_____

_____

_____

Were there any questions that were difficult for me to answer? If so, why?

_____

_____

_____

_____

Did my answers surprise me in any way? If so, why?

_____

_____

_____

_____

Is there anything else that occurs to me as I reflect upon what *being connected* looks like, feels like, or means in my life?

_____

_____

_____

_____

Feel free to use the following templates to help you to process your reflections.

Guided Reflection Flowchart Template

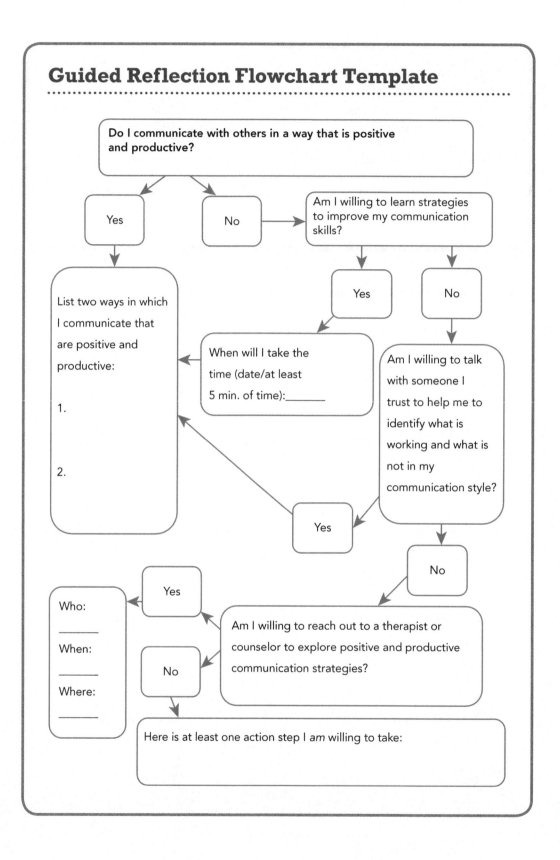

Do I communicate with others in a way that is positive and productive?

Yes

No → Am I willing to learn strategies to improve my communication skills?

Yes

No

List two ways in which I communicate that are positive and productive:

1.

2.

When will I take the time (date/at least 5 min. of time):_____

Am I willing to talk with someone I trust to help me to identify what is working and what is not in my communication style?

Yes

No

Who:

_____

When:

_____

Where:

_____

Yes

No

Am I willing to reach out to a therapist or counselor to explore positive and productive communication strategies?

Here is at least one action step I *am* willing to take:

Reflection Flowchart Template

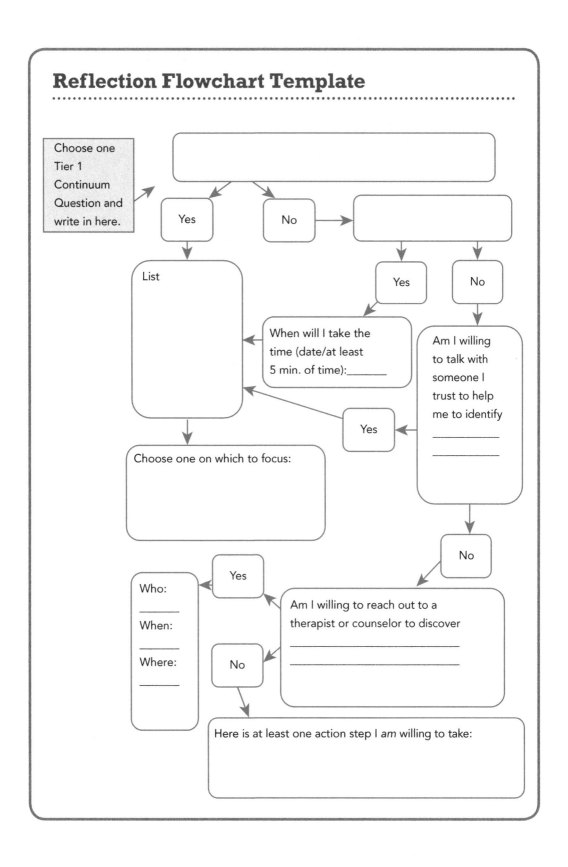

Choose one Tier 1 Continuum Question and write in here.

Yes

No

List

Yes

No

When will I take the time (date/at least 5 min. of time):_____

Am I willing to talk with someone I trust to help me to identify _____ _____

Yes

Choose one on which to focus:

No

Who: _____

When: _____

Where: _____

Yes

No

Am I willing to reach out to a therapist or counselor to discover _____ _____

Here is at least one action step I *am* willing to take:

Reflection Flowchart: Create Your Own

BE CONNECTED

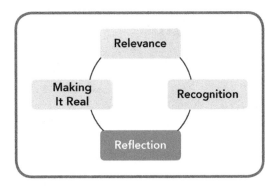

Relevance

Making It Real

Recognition

Reflection

Journaling Opportunity: Feel free to use the space below to write out any thoughts, reminders, "ahas," or curiosities that have occurred to you throughout the *Reflection* segment.

_____

_____

_____

_____

_____

_____

_____

_____

_____

_____

_____

_____

_____

_____

_____

_____

BE CONNECTED

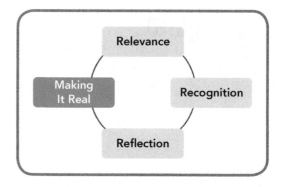

Prior to engaging in the Cultivation Challenge and Conscious Connection Challenge for being empathetic, I asked you to take one intentional breath. To lean into *Making It Real* for the Be Connected section, I'd like to ask you to stop reading and take a moment to write a note of appreciation to someone in your life. It may be someone you are close to, someone you sometimes inadvertently neglect to tell how much they mean to you, or you might choose a friend or acquaintance who makes a positive difference in your life. Regardless of who you select, limit your note to two to three sincere sentences and leave it somewhere for them to discover.

Thank you for taking time to engage in a practice of connection. Are you ready for your Cultivation Challenge?

Cultivation Challenge: Making It Real in Three, Two, One!

Three: Answer these three questions. (*Note*: Change "I" to "we" if accepting this challenge as a group.)

1. What is one area in which I have an opportunity for growth regarding my awareness or practice of being connected?

   _____

   _____

2. Why did I choose this area for growth?

   _____

   _____

   _____

   _____

3. If I were to grow or improve in this area, what would it make possible in my personal and/or professional life?

_____

_____

Two: List at least two ideas or ways that I might cultivate my opportunity for growth.

1. _____

   _____

   _____

2. _____

   _____

   _____

One: Choose one idea to apply. Use the Growth Action Plan table to record one idea, practice, and track and then celebrate or revise that idea or way to cultivate growth.

1. Growth Action Plan

OPPORTUNITY FOR GROWTH	PRACTICE	TRACK	CELEBRATE OR REVISE
List one idea or way to cultivate growth.	List one internal (thought/attitude) and one external (words, behaviors) element to practice.	Set a tangible goal for the week and tally the times per day you engage in practice.	Record a star or checkmark at the end of the week if your goal is met *or* revise your goal to scaffold your practice if necessary.
1.	1.	Goal:	Celebrate:
	2.	Tally:	Revise:

(Continued)

Though being connected may seem like an action that should occur naturally, we know that cultivating this way of being will help us make connections that matter. Thank you for taking time to accept this challenge! Now, the Conscious Connection Challenge awaits.

Conscious Connection Challenge: Be Connected

Step 1: Determine a desired outcome you would like to achieve in your personal or professional life.

Step 2: Define one conscious choice you *could* make in the realm of a specific way of being **connected** in order to achieve your desired outcome.

Step 3: Explain what it might look like if the outcome were to be achieved.

Step 4: List two to three emotions or feeling words that may be experienced if outcome were to be achieved.

Step 5: List one or two internal or subtle responses that may be present if outcome were to be achieved.

Conscious Connection Challenge: Follow the steps as you fill out the chart from right to left and consider the possibilities.

Life Situation: _____

	END ⬅ STEP 5	STEP 4 ⬅	STEP 3 ⬅	STEP 2 ⬅	START ⬅ STEP 1
LIFE SITUATION	**INTERNAL/ SUBTLE RESPONSES** (What this feels like inside)	**EMOTIONS/ FEELINGS** (What we experience based on emotions)	**EXTERNAL BEHAVIORS** (What this looks like)	**STRATEGIES** (A conscious choice we make to Be Connected)	**DESIRED OUTCOME**
Green Zone SOCIAL EMOTIONAL WELL-BEING					

BE CONNECTED

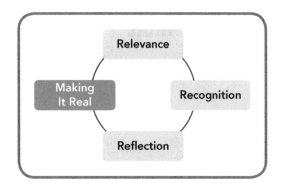

Journaling Opportunity: Feel free to use the space below to write out any thoughts, reminders, "ahas," or curiosities that have occurred to you throughout the *Making It Real* segment.

_____

_____

_____

_____

_____

_____

_____

_____

_____

_____

_____

_____

_____

_____

_____

_____

_____

_____

BE ACCOUNTABLE

To be accountable is to be reliable and worthy of trust. We have all experienced the disappointment that comes with a broken promise or abandoned commitment. It can damage relationships, negatively impact productivity, and cause frustration or regret. Accountability, on the other hand, is grounded in high expectations, dependability, and consistency. Being accountable to ourselves and others is a crucial element of the framework because to be accountable is to be responsible for our choices in thought, word, and deed. Being accountable can demonstrate integrity, relieve the burden of guilt, and repair harm. These acts, together or in and of themselves, support our social emotional well-being.

Throughout life, we make choices. Often, our choices are responsible, kind, and honorable. However, we have all experienced moments in our lives when we make a choice that does not represent our best selves. Poor choices can be made for a variety of reasons. Sometimes, the reason is simply related to growing up and searching for our own way to *be*. In teen years, we may not even recognize our choices are poor ones until we look back. Throughout adolescence *and* adulthood, our choices can be the result of carelessness, recklessness, or a quest for fun that does not take into account the potential consequences. Other times, we can be outright irresponsible—fueled by anger, frustration, greed, or fear. Or we may make a choice of which we are not proud to prove something, defend someone, or shift the blame. Consequently, regardless of our reasoning or lack thereof, our words and behaviors can cause unintended hurt or harm to ourselves or others.

Authentic accountability calls us to verbally own our transgressions, seek sincere forgiveness, and make concerted efforts to repair harm and to change our behavior. Each of these actions takes humility and courage. It is never easy to admit when we have done something or said something that negatively impacts ourselves or others. Yet when we admit our wrongs, it can bring peace to our lives and comfort, validation, or understanding to others.

Lastly, as educators we are responsible for addressing injustices and inequities within our school community. Being accountable means that we do not turn a blind eye when we see a student being bullied, nor do we shy away from opportunities to reflect upon our own potential bias thoughts or behaviors. Consequently, to be accountable is to be socially and culturally aware and responsive. Ultimately, it is solution-oriented and mindful of diversity and disproportionality. Accountability invites us to stand up for justice and that which is right.

I do realize that contemplating this way of being may feel overwhelming or intangible. Please remember as you consider the *Relevance* of what it means and looks like to Be Accountable and as you *Recognize*, *Reflect*, and *Make It Real*, that it is okay to take small steps or scaffold for yourself so that slowing leaning into this way of being is feasible, meaningful, and empowering.

BE ACCOUNTABLE

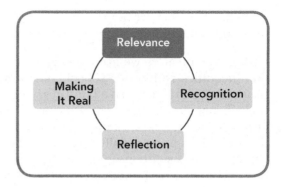

WHAT does it mean and look like to Be Accountable?

Being accountable means taking responsibility for our choices in thought, word, and deed. The primary focus includes, but is not limited to these actions:

- Being reliable
- Asking how our behavior impacts others
- Owning our poor choices or behavior
- Discovering, evaluating, and admitting our implicit and explicit biases
- Seeking sincere forgiveness by making amends
- Making efforts to change behavior that negatively impacts ourselves or others
- Being restorative to build community or restore harm
- Modeling responsible behavior choices and setting appropriate boundaries

WHY is it relevant to social emotional well-being?

- *Personal Relevance*: Being accountable relieves the burden of guilt. It helps us to practice humility and form more authentic relationships contributing to peace of heart, mind, and spirit.

- *Professional Relevance*: When we are accountable for our words, choices, and behaviors, we model responsible decision-making for our students, their families, and our colleagues, thus paving the way for others to follow our lead. Being accountable sustains relationships, encourages honesty, and demonstrates responsibility, influencing our ability to contribute to the collective good of our workplace.

SEL Connection: Responsible Decision-Making

BE ACCOUNTABLE

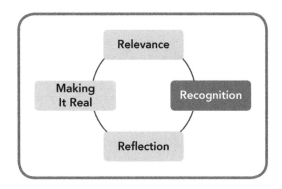

Within each way of being, we all possess specific qualities that support our social emotional well-being. Consider the statements from our Social Emotional Well-Being Check-In and highlight at least two strengths or add your own in the open spaces.

BE ACCOUNTABLE
I make responsible decisions.
I am reliable.
I make time to exercise at least three days per week in order to attend to my physical well-being.
I seek support when necessary to nourish my mental and/or emotional well-being.
I set boundaries that support my social emotional well-being.
I engage in at least one behavior per week that nurtures my spiritual well-being, such as praying, meditating, being in nature, or attending a religious ceremony.
I consider the impact of my choices on others when I make decisions.
I am culturally aware and responsive in my vocational practice.
I am ethically aware and responsive in my vocational practice.
I follow rules or protocols without exception.
I sincerely and verbally take responsibility for choices I make that negatively impact myself or others.
I seek sincere forgiveness when my words, attitudes, or behaviors negatively impact another.
I do the right thing, even when no one is watching.
I make a concerted effort to respond to situations from a place of love, as opposed to fear.
I take a stand against inequity and injustice.

Considering the row or two that you highlighted, or a strength you may have added, what does the practice of this way of being look like in your life?

_____

_____

_____

_____

How might the practice of your highlighted strength or strengths positively impact your well-being?

_____

_____

_____

_____

How might the practice of your highlighted strength or strengths positively impact those with whom you interact, care for, or love?

_____

_____

_____

_____

How might you leverage at least one of these strengths in order to provide an opportunity for another to feel valued or appreciated?

_____

_____

_____

_____

Recognition of our strengths in the realm of accountability matters because both human nature and the way in which were nurtured can cause us to carry guilt and judge ourselves harshly at times. In fact, one way we can be more accountable is to bestow the same forgiveness and grace to ourselves when we mess up that we would to a dear friend, family member, or student. We can also set boundaries for ourselves because when we are overwhelmed or take on responsibilities that are not ours to own, it can negatively impact our well-being. Perhaps you have mastered the art of setting boundaries and highlighted it as a strength. If not, might you consider this an opportunity for growth? Or might you focus on reliability or righting wrongs as a way in which to cultivate accountability? Regardless of what you choose, as we step into the *Reflection* section, I hope the wisdom of legendary coach, Pat Summit, will inspire your quest to be accountable.

BE ACCOUNTABLE

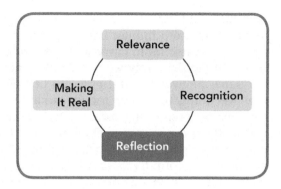

Pat Summitt was a celebrated women's basketball coach for the Tennessee Volunteers and an inspirational human being. Prior to her early-onset Alzheimer's diagnosis in 2011, followed by her death in 2016, she held the record as the winningest NCAA basketball coach of all time. That included men's *and* women's basketball! As a collegiate and US Olympic-winning coach, Pat Summit knew the value of accountability. She said, "Accountability is essential to personal growth, as well as team growth. How can you improve if you're never wrong? If you don't admit a mistake and take responsibility for it, you're bound to make the same one again."[5] Coach Summitt's wisdom was born of experience: a hard work ethic, a commitment to humanity, and an ambition to develop not only winning teams, but well-rounded, quality individuals.

As educators, we are individuals *and* we are a vital part of a team. Team growth and success require accountability. Coach Summit reminds us that if we cannot admit we are wrong, we cannot grow. Admitting a wrongdoing does not intimate weakness; it demonstrates integrity and promotes opportunities to grow. It also allows us to reflect on how our choices may impact others. Please use the Tiered Continuum of Questions to reflect on the various ways in which you might strive to be accountable.

---

[5]Pat Summitt and Sally Jenkins, *Reach for The Summit: The Definite Dozen System for Succeeding at Whatever You Do* (New York: Broadway Books, 1999), 39.

- Do I understand the definition of responsible decision-making?
- Do I make choices that enhance or support my physical, mental, emotional, and spiritual health and well-being?
- Do I make caring and constructive choices across diverse situations and contexts?
- Do I understand that practicing educational equity is vocationally responsible?
- Do I consider ethical standards, safety, equity, and the well-being of myself and others when I make choices?
- Do I use a constructive process to make decisions or solve a problem?
  - If so, do I collaborate with others in this process?
  - Do I consider the potential consequences (both positive and negative) of my decisions?
- Am I willing to be accountable for my own words or behaviors when I make a poor choice or when another is confused, hurt, or offended by me?
- Do I seek sincere forgiveness when my attitudes, words, or behaviors negatively impact another?
- Do I demonstrate integrity even when no one else may notice?
- Am I willing to stand up for and with others who are oppressed or treated in an unfair or unjust manner?

Be Accountable Tiered Continuum Self-Reflection Questions

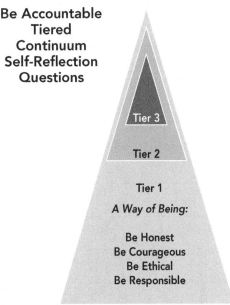

Tier 3

Tier 2

Tier 1

A Way of Being:

Be Honest
Be Courageous
Be Ethical
Be Responsible

© 2020 TruEd Consulting, LLC

Tier 2: Targeted Supports and/or Interventions

SOME of us may benefit from following up with these questions:

- Do I struggle with knowing how my decisions might impact others?
- Do I have difficulty determining how to create equitable learning opportunities or educational experiences for all students?
- Do I have difficulty recognizing and/or making the responsible choice in challenging or pressured situations?
- Would I benefit from small-group support or a workshop to focus on these items?
  - Effective decision-making strategies
  - Problem-solving skills
  - Resisting social pressure
  - Ethical decision-making

Tier 3: Intensive Individualized Supports and/or Interventions
A FEW of us may ask ourselves these questions:

- Does my lack of responsible decision-making negatively impact my relationships, and/or do I make choices that jeopardize my safety or the safety of others?
- Do I blame others to the point of never taking accountability for my actions?
- If I answered YES to either of these questions, might the support of a counselor, psychologist, or psychiatrist assist me in making more responsible choices?

BE ACCOUNTABLE

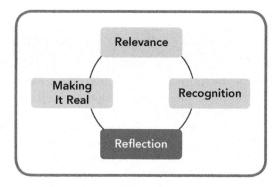

Please use the following question prompts to reflect upon how you live out being accountable and areas in which you might grow or improve this way of being in your life.

What do I notice about myself?

_____

_____

_____

_____

Were there any questions that were difficult for me to answer? If so, why?

_____

_____

_____

_____

Did my answers surprise me in any way? If so, why?

_____

_____

_____

_____

Is there anything else that occurs to me as I reflect upon what *being accountable* looks like, feels like, or means in my life?

_____

_____

_____

_____

Please use the following templates to help you to process your reflections.

Guided Reflection Flowchart Template

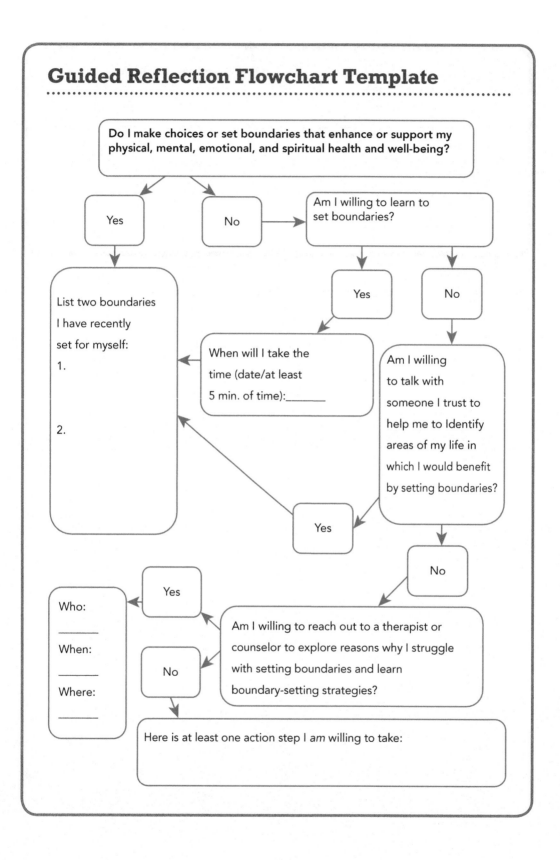

Do I make choices or set boundaries that enhance or support my physical, mental, emotional, and spiritual health and well-being?

Yes

No

Am I willing to learn to set boundaries?

List two boundaries I have recently set for myself:
1.

2.

Yes

No

When will I take the time (date/at least 5 min. of time):_____

Am I willing to talk with someone I trust to help me to Identify areas of my life in which I would benefit by setting boundaries?

Yes

No

Who:
_____
When:
_____
Where:
_____

Yes

No

Am I willing to reach out to a therapist or counselor to explore reasons why I struggle with setting boundaries and learn boundary-setting strategies?

Here is at least one action step I *am* willing to take:

Reflection Flowchart Template

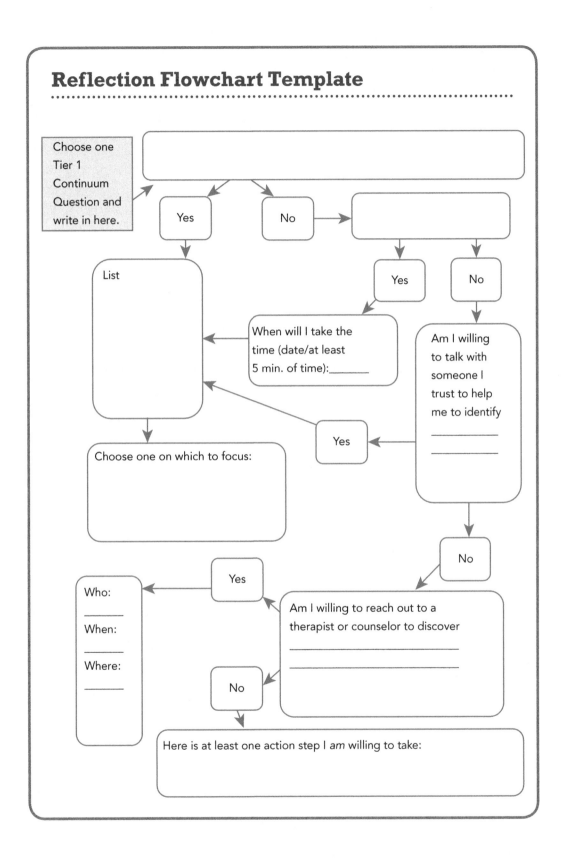

Choose one Tier 1 Continuum Question and write in here.

Yes

No

List

Yes

No

When will I take the time (date/at least 5 min. of time):_____

Am I willing to talk with someone I trust to help me to identify

_____

_____

Yes

Choose one on which to focus:

No

Yes

Am I willing to reach out to a therapist or counselor to discover

_____

_____

Who:

_____

When:

_____

Where:

_____

No

Here is at least one action step I *am* willing to take:

Reflection Flowchart: Create Your Own

BE ACCOUNTABLE

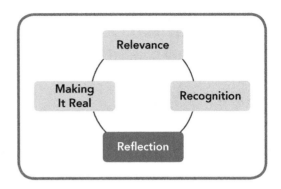

Journaling Opportunity: Feel free to use the space below to write out any thoughts, reminders, "ahas," or curiosities that have occurred to you throughout the *Reflection* segment.

_____

_____

_____

_____

_____

_____

_____

_____

_____

_____

_____

_____

_____

_____

BE ACCOUNTABLE

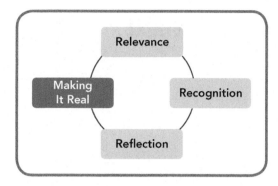

The *Be Accountable* Cultivation and Conscious Connection Challenges call for us to access the universal accountability behaviors of being honest, courageous, ethical, and responsible. We may also want to consider a challenge to be accountable for ourselves and another to be accountable to others. Both are valuable ways of being that nourish our social emotional well-being. Please engage in making it real, beginning with our Cultivation Challenge.

Cultivation Challenge: Making It Real in Three, Two, One!

Three: Answer these three questions. (*Note*: Change "I" to "we" if accepting this challenge as a group.)

1. What is one area in which I have an opportunity for growth regarding my awareness or practice of being connected?

    _____

    _____

2. Why did I choose this area for growth?

    _____

    _____

    _____

    _____

3. If I were to grow or improve in this area, what would it make possible in my personal and/ or professional life?

_____

_____

_____

_____

Two: List at least two ideas or ways that I might cultivate my opportunity for growth.

1. _____

_____

_____

2. _____

_____

_____

One: Choose one idea to apply. Use the Growth Action Plan table to record one idea, practice, and track and then celebrate or revise that idea or way to cultivate growth.

1. Growth Action Plan

OPPORTUNITY FOR GROWTH	PRACTICE	TRACK	CELEBRATE OR REVISE
List one idea or way to cultivate growth.	List one internal (thought/attitude) and one external (words, behaviors) element to practice.	Set a tangible goal for the week and tally the times per day you engage in practice.	Record a star or checkmark at the end of the week if your goal is met *or* revise your goal to scaffold your practice if necessary.
1.	1.	Goal:	Celebrate:
	2.	Tally:	Revise:

Thank you for creating an action plan to be more accountable. Please stay dedicated to practicing, tracking, celebrating, or revising your chosen idea or way to cultivate growth so that you can reap the rewards of being accountable. Please take a moment to stand up, touch three walls of the physical space within which you are reading, and focus your eyes upon something that brings you joy, before you move on to our Conscious Connection Challenge.

Conscious Connection Challenge: Be Accountable

Step 1: Determine a desired outcome you would like to achieve in your personal or professional life.

Step 2: Define one conscious choice you *could* make in the realm of a specific way of being <u>accountable</u> in order to achieve your desired outcome.

Step 3: Explain what it might look like if the outcome were to be achieved.

Step 4: List two to three emotions or feeling words that may be experienced if outcome were to be achieved.

Step 5: List one or two internal or subtle responses that may be present if outcome were to be achieved.

Conscious Connection Challenge: Follow the steps as you fill out the chart from right to left and consider the possibilities.

Life Situation: _____

	END STEP 5	STEP 4	STEP 3	STEP 2	START STEP 1
LIFE SITUATION	**INTERNAL/ SUBTLE RESPONSES** (What this feels like inside)	**EMOTIONS/ FEELINGS** (What we experience based on emotions)	**EXTERNAL BEHAVIORS** (What this looks like)	**STRATEGIES** (A conscious choice we make to Be Accountable)	**DESIRED OUTCOME**
Green Zone SOCIAL EMOTIONAL WELL-BEING					

BE ACCOUNTABLE

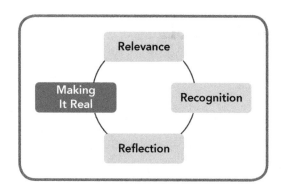

Journaling Opportunity: Feel free to use the space below to write out any thoughts, reminders, "ahas," or curiosities that have occurred to you throughout the *Making It Real* segment.

_____

_____

_____

_____

_____

_____

_____

_____

_____

_____

_____

_____

_____

_____

_____

_____

BE EQUITABLE

There is much talk today about the need to Be Equitable, as well as the long-overdue call to action to address systemic racism. Issues related to equity, or lack thereof, have been present in society, as well as in the educational system, for generations. As I reflect, it is disheartening to acknowledge that it took the tragic murder of George Floyd and the disparities in resources and accessibility that were revealed by the pandemic to catalyze a more authentic equity movement within society and education.

As educators, we know our system is notorious for talking about the importance of equity, yet we must ask this imperative question: Does our walk match our talk? Though there are a handful of activists and advocates actively engaged in doing intensive equity and diversity work, there are more of us who tend to be unsure about *how* to actually address disproportionality, diversity, racism, and social injustice. My colleague Kori Hamilton Biagas, founder of Just Educators, offers the following definition of equity: "Equity is being invited to dinner *and* given a seat at the table."[6] When I first read her definition, I couldn't help but reflect on my own vocational practice. In my enthusiastic offering of the invitation, did I neglect to set a place at the table? For some students, without even realizing it, I'm sure I did. Being authentic in our pursuit to be equitable must begin with genuinely walking our talk. The first step requires that we look within.

We must ask ourselves tough questions about the ways in which we make assumptions or judgments of other people. I know that some of you may be thinking, "I don't do that. I make a point not to judge." And though you may try, the reality is that we all make judgments. We judge or assume things based on how someone looks, what they say, how they dress, and what they do. We assume good and bad; we judge right or wrong. We make these presumptions using the only schema we have: our own experiences.

[6]Kori Hamilton Biagas, written interview response to Michelle L. Trujillo, March 2021.

To be equitable, we must be willing to look at our own implicit biases. I realize "implicit" suggests that we don't even know they are there— which is why we must accept that we don't know what we don't know and strive to increase our awareness. We can do this by engaging in an implicit bias evaluation, such as Harvard's Implicit Association Test, which can be found at https://implicit.harvard.edu/implicit/ takeatest.html. We can reflect on our personal and ancestral stories that may have led to our understanding, or our misunderstandings, of the world around us. And we can step into the discomfort of learning more about those whose race, ethnicity, gender, ability, religion, or socioeconomic status differ from our own. Furthermore, our social emotional well-being will be stretched in ways that grow our hearts and minds if we have the courage to identify our explicit biases as well. These are prejudices we knowingly project. Consequently, biases, implicit or explicit, result in disregarding equity.

With open hearts and minds, we will begin to understand that equity and equality are not the same. As an administrator, I often reminded my students that fair is not equal. Equal means that everyone gets the same thing and is treated in the same way. Equality typically refers to what is being offered, whereas equity considers the human receiving what is being offered. Being equitable educators requires that we ensure every student has what he, she, or they need to be physically, socially, emotionally, and academically engaged in school. Thus, being equitable means providing for our students according to their circumstance by addressing potential barriers to learning, such as poverty, lack of health care, or limited transportation.

Finally, being equitable also requires that we study historical and systemic oppression because we cannot disrupt norms that contribute to inequitable practices if we don't understand their origin.

According to the National Museum of African American History and Culture,

> "Oppression" refers to a combination of prejudice and institutional power that creates a system that regularly and severely discriminates against some groups and benefits other groups. . . . The term "systems of oppression" helps us better identify inequity by calling attention to the historical and organized patterns of mistreatment. In the United States, systems of oppression (like systemic racism) are woven into the very foundation of American culture, society, and laws. Other examples of systems of oppression are sexism, heterosexism, ableism, classism, ageism, and anti-Semitism. Society's institutions, such as government, education, and culture, all contribute or reinforce the oppression of marginalized social groups while elevating dominant social groups.[7]

---

[7]National Museum of African American History and Culture, "Social Identities and Systems of Oppression," July 17, 2020, nmaahc.si.edu/learn/ talking-about-race/topics/social-identities-and-systems-oppression.

I realize that some of us may read the definition of oppression and understand it all too well because we've experienced oppression ourselves. Others of us, however, come from a place of privilege, whether we want to admit it or not, and we will never truly understand what it is to be oppressed. Regardless, Dena Simmons, activist and founder of LiberatED, implores educators to use our own social emotional skills to step into "courageous conversations across difference" with our students, even if we don't know quite what to say. According to Simmons, "We can no longer avoid discussing topics that make us uncomfortable. Our students, incessantly inundated with divisive rhetoric and reports of premeditated acts of violence (or even themselves targets of violence), don't have that luxury."[8] It is essential that we access all of our ways of being—reflective, intentional, empathetic, connected, and accountable—as we endeavor to make certain that situations and systems are equitable for those in our care.

---

[8]Dena Simmons, "Why We Can't Afford Whitewashed Social-Emotional Learning," *ASCD*, April 1, 2019, https://www.ascd.org/el/articles/why-we-cant-afford-whitewashed-social-emotional-learning.

BE EQUITABLE

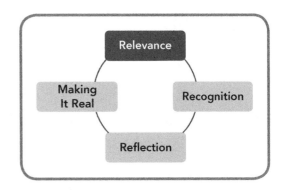

WHAT does it mean and look like to Be Equitable?

Being equitable means being fair, just, and free from bias. Primary focus includes but is not limited to these actions:

- Understanding that fair is not equal
- Putting systems in place to ensure equitable accessibility and opportunity for all
- Discovering and mitigating educational disparities
- Understanding the unique needs, challenges, and barriers of every individual
- Addressing and disrupting social and racial injustice and inequity—in word and deed

WHY is it relevant to social emotional well-being?

- *Personal Relevance*: Being equitable instigates personal social emotional growth because it requires that we learn about the traditions, cultures, and ways of being of others. This growth helps us to be more understanding and well-rounded individuals.

- *Professional Relevance*: Being equitable helps us to create inclusive classroom environments and to honor all individuals within the school community, thus fostering an accepting, fair, and just school culture. Contributing to the creation of such an environment can lead to vocational gratification and purpose.

SEL Connection: Responsible Decision-Making

BE EQUITABLE

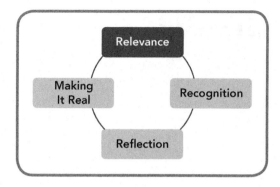

Being equitable requires introspection. Use this attribute as you consider the statements from our Social Emotional Well-Being Check-In. For our final way of being, please identify two strengths you possess, or feel free to add in statements that represent your strengths in being equitable to the bottom of the list.

BE EQUITABLE
I recognize my own explicit biases.
I recognize my own implicit biases.
I honor and respect the language, customs, and cultural norms of others.
I understand historical and systemic inequities based on race, ethnicity, gender, ability, religion, socioeconomic status, and more.
I respectfully engage in conversations with others whose cultural experiences differ from my own in order to learn, grow, and act in a fair and impartial manner.
I notice and respectfully confront injustice and/or inequities.
I set high expectations and provide high support for *all* students (and staff).
I consider the needs of *all* students (or staff) when designing instruction or making decisions.
I differentiate instruction or activities to meet the needs of *all* learners.
I consider accessibility barriers and make necessary modifications when assigning tasks or homework.
I create opportunities to learn about the customs, traditions, and ways of being of others.

Considering the row or two that you highlighted, or a strength you may have added, what does the practice of this way of being look like in your life?

_____

_____

_____

_____

How might the practice of your highlighted strength or strengths positively impact your well-being?

_____

_____

_____

_____

How might the practice of your highlighted strength or strengths positively impact those with whom you interact, care for, or love?

_____

_____

_____

_____

How might you leverage at least one of these strengths in order to provide an opportunity for another to feel valued or appreciated?

_____

_____

_____

_____

Be Equitable is the last puzzle piece of our framework—not because it is least important, but because it requires that we engage all of our ways of being in order to be equitable with authenticity. As you identified and reflected upon your strengths related to being equitable, I wonder if you recognized that you also accessed other ways of being? If so, please indicate your thoughts here:

_____

_____

_____

As we begin our final *Reflection* section, please take a moment to think back on the story of your life, your family. Where are your ancestral roots? What customs or traditions do you practice today that have origins in your heritage? What is the first thing that comes to mind?

_____

_____

_____

_____

_____

_____

Keep your answers in your thoughts as we reflect on ways in which we might become more equitable.

BE EQUITABLE

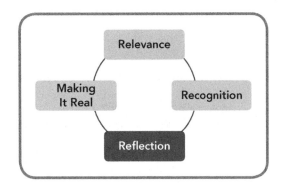

I asked you to reflect on your own ancestral story because when we contemplate areas in which we might grow in our pursuit of being equitable educators, our own stories are a place from which we can appreciate, honor, learn, and grow.

I appear to be a white, middle-class educator. However, my primary ethnic identity is Middle Eastern. My impatience, persistence, enthusiasm for food, and love of family come, in great part, from my ancestry. My great-aunts were fiercely independent women who came to America determined to prosper. Stories of their work ethic, business acumen, and conquests inspire me. My grandfather, an industrious attorney, was a survivor of polio and found joy in preparing traditional Syrian dishes. I remember watching him in the kitchen as he ground lamb for Kibbeh Nayyeh or Yebra—my mouth watering, my eyes focusing on the smile in my Bapa's eyes, and my ears listening to the songs he would sing as he cranked the handle on the grinder.

Anyone who looks at me on the outside would not know this about me. It is my story, and unless someone asks, they likely would not know. I share this with you because as much as I identify with my *own* ancestral roots, as a white teacher I will not know or understand the experiences, customs, or stories of my Black or brown students. I must draw from what I know about myself and then open my heart and mind to what I do not know about others. This is something we all can do. Perhaps our final Continuum of Questions may provide insight into ways in which we may become more equitable.

Tier 1: Universal Practices
We can ALL ask these questions:

- Do I understand the definition of educational equity?
- Do I pursue opportunities to learn about my own potential biases, both implicit and explicit?
- Do I understand what it means to be equitable in words, attitudes, and behaviors?
- Do I pursue opportunities to learn about historical and systemic inequities based on race, gender, ability, religion, socioeconomic status, and more?
  - o If so, what do I do to cultivate opportunities for equity?

AND

  - o Do I consider and, furthermore, deconstruct expectations, cultural norms of schooling, and ways of interacting to expand my view of success and normative behavior to include the experiences, cultural ways of knowing, and aspirations of students of color and their families?
- Do I consider the needs of *all* students, including those whose race, gender, ability, religion, and socioeconomic status differ from my own?
- Am I aware of the community resources available to students and families within my school community?
- Am I aware of how my students get to and from school?

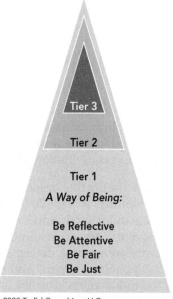

Be Equitable Tiered Continuum Self-Reflection Questions

Tier 3

Tier 2

Tier 1

A Way of Being:

Be Reflective
Be Attentive
Be Fair
Be Just

© 2020 TruEd Consulting, LLC

Tier 2: Targeted Supports and/or Interventions
SOME of us may benefit from following up with these questions:

- Do I have difficulty determining how to create equitable learning opportunities or educational experiences for all students?
- Would I benefit from a workshop, course, or training to learn more about these issues?
  - o Educational equity and diversity
  - o Social and/or racial justice and/or antiracism
  - o Diverse learners or ability equity
  - o Racial, gender, or socioeconomic disparities
  - o Implicit bias awareness
  - o Antiracist instructional strategies
- Do my implicit biases show up explicitly, and might a workshop, training, or course help me to be more responsible?
- Is there a workshop or training available that would help me to deconstruct cultural norms of schooling and ways of interacting to expand my view of success and normative behavior to include the experiences, cultural ways of knowing, and aspirations of students of color and their families?

Tier 3: Intensive Individualized Supports and/or Interventions
A FEW of us may ask ourselves these questions:

- Do my choices lead to injustice or inequity?
- Have I ever been told by a trusted friend or colleague that I am biased? Have I reflected on that information with genuine curiosity and a desire to understand my biases?
- If I answered YES to any of these questions, might it help to seek the support of a counselor, psychologist, or psychiatrist to guide me in becoming more socially aware?

BE EQUITABLE

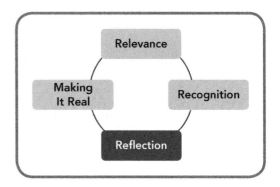

Relevance

Recognition

Reflection

Making It Real

Please use the following question prompts to reflect upon how you live out being equitable, as well as ways in which you might grow or improve your quest to be equitable.

What do I notice about myself?

_____

_____

_____

_____

Were there any questions that were difficult for me to answer? If so, why?

_____

_____

_____

_____

Did my answers surprise me in any way? If so, why?

_____

_____

_____

_____

(Continued)

(Continued)

Is there anything else that occurs to me as I reflect upon what *being equitable* looks like, feels like, or means in my life?

_____

_____

_____

_____

At this point, you have likely determined which of the following templates help you to process your reflections. Feel free to use that which works best for you.

Guided Reflection Flowchart Template

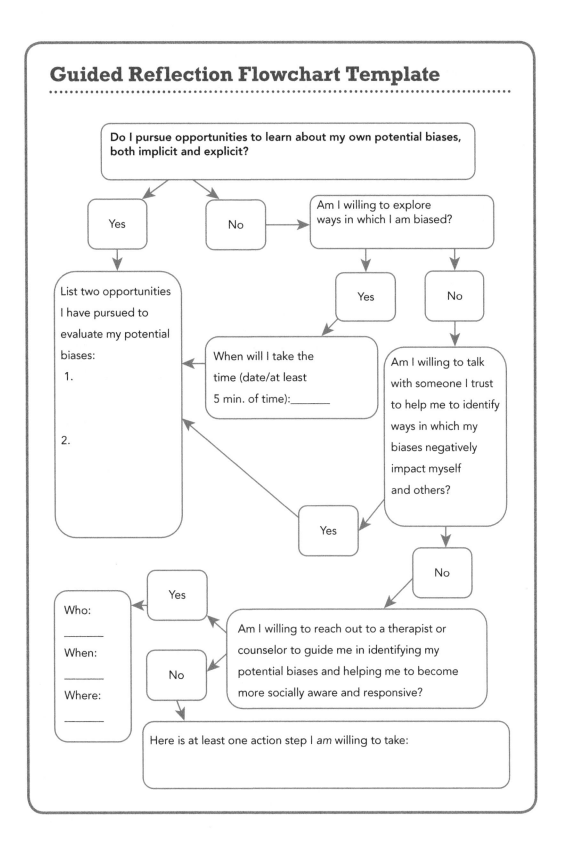

Do I pursue opportunities to learn about my own potential biases, both implicit and explicit?

Yes

No

Am I willing to explore ways in which I am biased?

Yes

No

List two opportunities I have pursued to evaluate my potential biases:

1.

2.

When will I take the time (date/at least 5 min. of time):_____

Am I willing to talk with someone I trust to help me to identify ways in which my biases negatively impact myself and others?

Yes

No

Who:
_____
When:
_____
Where:
_____

Yes

No

Am I willing to reach out to a therapist or counselor to guide me in identifying my potential biases and helping me to become more socially aware and responsive?

Here is at least one action step I *am* willing to take:

Reflection Flowchart Template

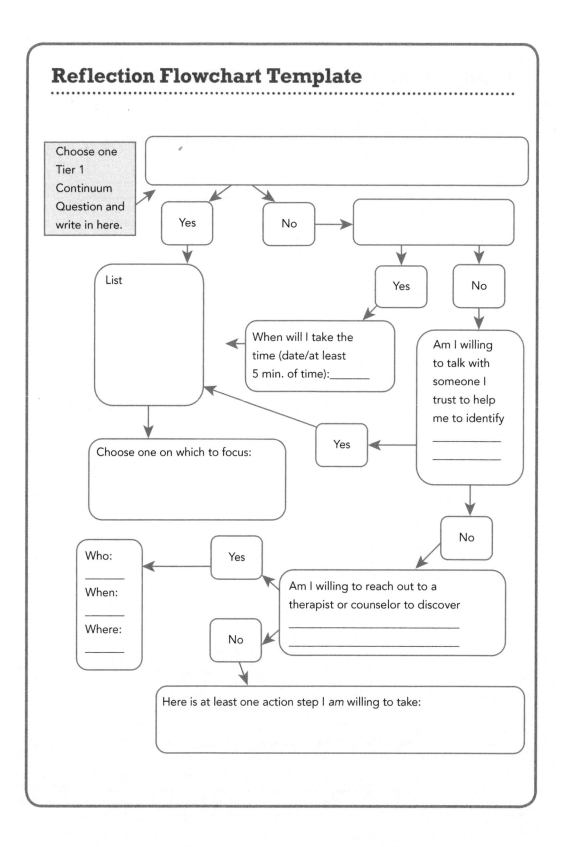

Choose one Tier 1 Continuum Question and write in here.

Yes

No

List

Yes

No

When will I take the time (date/at least 5 min. of time):_____

Am I willing to talk with someone I trust to help me to identify _____ _____

Yes

Choose one on which to focus:

No

Who: _____
When: _____
Where: _____

Yes

No

Am I willing to reach out to a therapist or counselor to discover _____ _____

Here is at least one action step I *am* willing to take:

Reflection Flowchart: Create Your Own

BE EQUITABLE

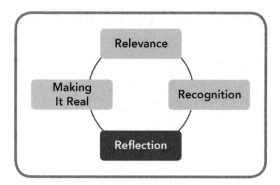

Journaling Opportunity: Feel free to use the space below to write out any thoughts, reminders, "ahas," or curiosities that have occurred to you throughout the *Reflection* segment.

_____

_____

_____

_____

_____

_____

_____

_____

_____

_____

_____

_____

_____

_____

_____

_____

_____

BE EQUITABLE

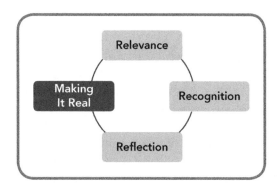

Prior to engaging in our final Cultivation Challenge and Conscious Connection Challenge for being equitable, I want to ask you to think about the little things—our use of words, for example. Do we refer to a "homeless student" or a "student currently living in transition?" Do we say, "Down's student, SPED student, Tier 3 student," or do we say, "student with Down syndrome, student eligible for special education, or student receiving Tier 3 interventions and supports"? The ways in which we use our words matter and contribute to our efforts in being equitable. When we place the word "student" first, then the human being—rather than the label—becomes our primary focus. This small example brings us full circle and back to a *way of being*. Using words to express ourselves is something we already do; *how* we use those words, however, can impact our social emotional well-being by providing opportunities for us to be intentional, connected, and equitable.

As you engage in your final Cultivation and Conscious Connection Challenges, feel free to incorporate any and all of our ways of being in your pursuit of cultivating equity.

Cultivation Challenge: Making It Real in Three, Two, One!

Three: Answer these three questions. (*Note:* Change "I" to "we" if accepting this challenge as a group.)

1. What is one area in which I have an opportunity for growth regarding my awareness or practice of being equitable?

_____

_____

(Continued)

(Continued)

_____

_____

2. Why did I choose this area for growth?

_____

_____

_____

_____

3. If I were to grow or improve in this area, what would it make possible in my personal and/
   or professional life?

_____

_____

_____

_____

Two: List at least two ideas or ways that I might cultivate my opportunity for growth.

1. _____

_____

_____

2. _____

_____

_____

One: Choose one idea to apply. Use the Growth Action Plan table to record one idea, practice, and track and then celebrate or revise that idea or way to cultivate growth.

1. Growth Action Plan

OPPORTUNITY FOR GROWTH	PRACTICE	TRACK	CELEBRATE OR REVISE
List one idea or way to cultivate growth.	List one internal (thought/attitude) and one external (words, behaviors) element to practice.	Set a tangible goal for the week and tally the times per day you engage in practice.	Record a star or checkmark at the end of the week if your goal is met or revise your goal to scaffold your practice if necessary.
1.	1.	Goal:	Celebrate:
	2.	Tally:	Revise:

Conscious Connection Challenge: Be Equitable

Conscious Connection Challenge: Follow the steps as you fill out the chart from right to left and consider the possibilities.

Life Situation: _____

Step 1: Determine a desired outcome you would like to achieve in your personal or professional life.

Step 2: Define one conscious choice you *could* make in the realm of a specific way of being **connected** in order to achieve your desired outcome.

Step 3: Explain what it might look like if the outcome were to be achieved.

Step 4: List two to three emotions or feeling words that may be experienced if outcome were to be achieved.

(Continued)

(Continued)

Step 5: List one or two internal or subtle responses that may be present if outcome were to be achieved.

	END STEP 5 ←	STEP 4 ←	STEP 3 ←	STEP 2 ←	START STEP 1 ←
LIFE SITUATION	**INTERNAL/ SUBTLE RESPONSES** (What this feels like inside)	**EMOTIONS/ FEELINGS** (What we experience based on emotions)	**EXTERNAL BEHAVIORS** (What this looks like)	**STRATEGIES** (A conscious choice we make to Be Equitable)	**DESIRED OUTCOME**
Green Zone SOCIAL EMOTIONAL WELL-BEING					

BE EQUITABLE

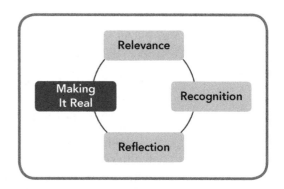

Journaling Opportunity: Feel free to use the space below to write out any thoughts, reminders, "ahas," or curiosities that have occurred to you throughout the *Making It Real* segment.

_____

_____

_____

_____

_____

_____

_____

_____

_____

_____

_____

_____

_____

_____

Whew! We just completed our final piece of the Framework for Social Emotional Well-Being. For each way of being, we identified *Relevance*, took time to *Recognize* strengths and *Reflect* on ways in which we might grow, and we engaged in *Making It Real* by accepting challenges to cultivate positive impact. I hope you have come to appreciate that each way of being can nourish and enhance our social emotional well-being.

I asked much of you as you applied each exercise to your own realm of experience, need, and opportunity. Thank you for engaging in reflections and challenges. Thank you for keeping an open mind and an open heart. Thank you for sharing what you have experienced through your reading and activities with others and for initiating conversations regarding ideas that you don't understand or those with which you don't agree. It is through all of these practices that we learn, grow, and model for others.

Modeling words, attitudes, choices, and behaviors that nurture our well-being is one of the most valuable ways we, as educators, can "teach" our students. Regardless of the role we serve in education, we are models, especially when challenged with adversity. As such, I would like to offer you a final resource as we near the end of *Social Emotional Well-Being for Educators*. It is a guidance document for modeling in the moment. I initially created it at the peak of the pandemic, when educators were confused, frustrated, and uncertain about what the future held. I have modified it a bit and share it with you now, knowing that although the book will be available as we enter what some are referring to as a post–COVID-19 era, many of us may still be serving students through a distance or hybrid approach. None of us truly knows what the future will hold, yet we do know we have the tools necessary to meet it with grace and confidence.

MODELING IN THE MOMENT

Educators realize that our every action is observed, often analyzed, and sometimes imitated by our students. Whether we want the responsibility or not, we model a way of being every moment through our attitudes, words, and behaviors. When our vocational calling becomes challenging due to situations that are out of our control, it is especially important that we are deliberate in our way of being. Thus, I have created the **Guidance for *Being* During Distance or Hybrid Education**, which includes specific ideas for each way of being. Each way of being is aligned with a specific social emotional learning competency. I realize you may wonder why I waited until the end of the book to provide these ideas. Please know that it was intentional. I wanted you to draw from your own strengths, creativity, curiosity, and quest for growth before I led you to specific suggestions, ideas, or strategies. Also, this guidance document is meant to be applied specifically to living and working through distance or hybrid education, while the Framework for Social Emotional Well-Being, on which we spent the majority of our focus, can be applied to our daily lives regardless of where or how we serve our vocations.

As you review the Guidance for *Being* During Distance or Hybrid Education, please highlight a bullet point within each way of being that resonates with you from your own way of being during the beginning of the pandemic. Underline a bullet point that you might put into practice today, regardless of whether we are dealing with challenges related to the pandemic. And draw a star or asterisk to the left of a bullet point that you would like to work toward integrating into your life and way of being in the future.

Guidance for *Being* During
Distance or Hybrid Education

> ## BE REFLECTIVE
> ## (FOCUS: SELF-AWARENESS)
>
> - Notice when you begin to feel overwhelmed or frustrated regarding an inability to deliver instruction the way in which you are accustomed, and as famous basketball coach, John Wooden, suggests, "Don't let what you cannot do interfere with what you can do." So take a deep breath and reflect on attitudes and behaviors that *are* in your control.
>
> - It is okay to acknowledge that this moment in time is challenging! Notice when you begin to feel anxious or discouraged and remind yourself that "this too shall pass." In the meantime, know that it is reasonable to feel whatever you are feeling. Give yourself time to sit with that feeling or verbalize that feeling. There is something about verbalizing an anxiety, concern, or fear that releases the burden a bit. At the same time, acknowledge that in this moment there are valuable lessons about life for you, your students, and/or your own children to learn. With your family or your students, reflect on some of these lessons through conversation, writing, or drawing.
>
> - Acknowledge your strengths. There are character strengths you possess that will serve you well as you take on your personal and professional responsibilities. Name them. Let them empower you to make a positive difference in your own life and the lives of others. Help your students or your own children to recognize a strength they possess and discuss how that strength may contribute to resilience during adversity.
>
> - There will be times when you will feel that everyone wants a piece of you: your spouse or partner, your kids, your parents, your students, or their families . . . you know who they are. Create a "peace place" for yourself and suggest your family, friends, and students do the same. When you notice that you are beginning to feel the demands of others overtaking your sanity and serenity, take time to retreat—if only for a few minutes. Take time to breathe, meditate, pray, or read in this place. You are allowed to relax and refresh; in fact, it is necessary that you do so.
>
> - I heard the term "radical self-acceptance" referred to quite often during the height of the pandemic. This may be the most valuable self-awareness or reflection strategy to practice. We are living in a moment with ourselves and our loved ones in which much is out of our control. If and when we accept this, we can begin to put one foot in front of the other, realizing that there is no "right" way to do this. We get to accept ourselves and our path in this moment and choose to make the most of it. When we accept the reality of our current living and working situation, we will be more able to see the blessing of creating a path through it that honors our family values and our professional growth.
>
> - Be aware of situations that inspire laughter, such as virtual gatherings with family and friends, funny videos or social media posts, or watching sitcoms on television or comedy movies on your computer. Seek these situations, for laughter is healthy for the body and soul.

BE INTENTIONAL
(FOCUS: SELF-MANAGEMENT)

- There was much guidance given to educators during the pandemic related to lowering expectations in an effort to give ourselves grace. Grace serves us well in this moment, and thus, I would encourage you to take a different perspective. Set *high* expectations for yourself in areas that you might typically find challenging, such as patience, flexibility, or being still. Use this "growth mindset" shift as a lesson to share with your students or with your own children.

- We often hear, or even use, the term "learning loss." Remember that our students (and you and I too) have learned much during the pandemic—valuable life lessons. If there is a loss related to education, it is a loss in instructional time. Be intentional in choosing to focus on instruction versus learning when referencing time away from traditional instruction.

- One of the benefits of living in the realization that so much is out of our control is that we have an opportunity to reflect on those choices that *are* within our control. One such choice is that of nourishing ourselves well. Grocery shopping may take planning if you are ordering online, as there tends to be a lapse of time between order and pick-up/delivery, but it is very much in our control to order foods that are nutritious. We can also choose to use food preparation as a time to unwind, be creative, or cook with the family. At the same time, there is nothing wrong with throwing in a treat every now and then!

- Movement is good! We know that our students are more productive when they have opportunities to move at incremental times during instruction. We will benefit from practicing this ourselves. Plan 15 minutes of movement for every 45 minutes that you are sedentary. I have also discovered that starting the day with at least 30 minutes of exercise gives me more energy with which to tackle what lies ahead.

- It would be very easy to live in our pajamas, sweats, or yoga pants during the time that we teach or work from home. However, there is much truth to the fact that our dress can influence the way we act. Creating a work-from-home schedule that includes a time to shower and dress for "work" may help to delineate between the time to work and the time to play, rest, exercise, or enjoy your family.

- As educators, we all know that students and adults alike can become dependent on or addicted to our electronic devices. Because our phones and computers give us constant updates and feedback, we can be drawn in and often distracted by social media, the news, and the constant barrage of sad and discouraging information. If we choose to limit the amount of time we spend on our devices, we may find our outlook on life and the future is more positive. Note that I am not advocating complete detachment because we must stay informed in order to make wise choices, and we can learn a great deal from reputable, data-based websites.

- Breathing techniques or mindfulness strategies have been known to help our students by improving focus and concentration and decreasing anxiety. Likewise, these practices can help us to experience calm and be more attentive to our tasks while working from home. One evidence-based approach that I have found to have helpful resources can be found at www.pureedgeinc.org. The Collaborative of Academic, Social and Emotional Learning also has a number of self-management resources for educators that can be found at www.CASEL.org.

BE EMPATHETIC
(FOCUS: SOCIAL AWARENESS)

- Look for the good around you. There were so many human beings working on the front lines during the pandemic who served others with great compassion and conviction and without an ounce of complaint. Recognize an individual or group of people who continue to make a positive impact by sending saying thank you and finding a way to intentionally pay it forward.

- Notice the ways in which people appreciate each other. During the "stay at home" phase of the pandemic, I observed a friendly nature in neighbors (from a distance, of course) that wasn't as prevalent in the busyness of what *was* our lives prepandemic. I noticed people waving greetings across the street, shouting words of encouragement, and offering to assist neighbors in need. Families began taking time to sit down for meals, praying, learning, and growing together. As traumatic and tragic as the pain of this pandemic has been, as much loss as we have experienced, we have also gained. We have gained perspective of that which is truly important: our humanity.

- I read many articles reminding educators of our privilege during the pandemic—that many people were able to stay home and work from home; that we were safe, warm, educated, and well-fed; that we enjoyed quality family time, exercise, rest, or reading. I am grateful for these reminders and hope that as we consider our own lives through this lens, we also remember that there are so many students who found their safety and security at school. When teaching or working through distance or hybrid education, let's do everything we can to stay emotionally connected to our students and their families—by eliminating barriers that limit their learning. Distance education has shined a spotlight on the true inequities in the educational system. Use this time as an opportunity to peer through the eyes of one who may not be living in the reality of privilege, safety, or security. Furthermore, learn about racism. Many of our students, their families, and some of our colleagues have experienced the reality of oppression throughout their lives. With intentionality, challenge yourself to better understand the root causes of the opportunity gaps experienced by some of our students and commit to apply this understanding to your educational practice. Furthermore, discover ways in which you can become part of the solution by disrupting inequities within the educational system, despite distance, hybrid, or in-person learning.

- Consider those who have lost their income. Some of us frequent favorite restaurants, can afford to employ someone to clean our house, or spend money on our hair or nails. While we are potentially saving money by eliminating these activities during this pandemic, many of the people who provide these services have gone without. If you are able and have not returned to your "normal" routines yet, consider continuing to contribute what you have budgeted for your hair, massage, nails, or outings to the person or people who have lost such income.

- Finally, assume the best in others. People may do things or say things that we don't agree with or understand. Before we jump to conclusions or make judgments, let's practice patience, tolerance, and forgiveness. It's possible that people who act angry, rude, or mean may be feeling uncertain, frustrated, helpless, or hopeless. This is the perfect time to seek to understand, to listen more, and to come from a place of love in our thoughts and our actions.

BE CONNECTED
(FOCUS: RELATIONSHIP SKILLS)

- We all know the power of physical connection. When we physically connect with another human being, we actually get a release of a chemical in our brain called oxytocin, which makes us feel good. Unfortunately, to protect ourselves and others, casual contact with neighbors and friends may still be extremely dangerous, especially if we are not vaccinated or those with whom we are in contact are not. As such, we must make emotional and social connection a priority.

- Greet people using their names, smile authentically, and if it is necessary to wear a mask in a given situation, verbally express what you are feeling. There is so much we can learn or understand about how a person feels from the expressions on their face. If a mask is covering our face, we may need to articulate our feelings to better connect with others.

- Reach out to others. Take time to call an elderly neighbor or someone who you know lives alone to check in, if only to say hello. It is difficult to be cooped up inside without that ability to interact with others. Sometimes, just hearing someone's voice or words of encouragement can bring hope. The same can be said for our students who may not be turning in work or showing up for virtual classes. We don't have to simply accept that they chose not to show; we can make an effort to speak with them in person by phone or send them a postcard of encouragement or a small token of compassion in the mail—just to let them know that connection is important to you and that you aren't going anywhere.

- Begin to use the term "physical distancing" instead of "social distancing." This accomplishes two goals. It helps us to emphasize the importance of staying physically distant from each other while this virus is rampant. It also recognizes the importance of staying socially connected, even while we are physically separated. We can remain socially connected by making an effort to stay in touch. We can use social media to play games, share ideas, and interact with one another. I realize it is not the same as prepandemic, but if we make an effort, our relations can grow.

- Grow more intentional relationships with those with whom you are closest. Sometimes in the fast pace of our typical routines, we unintentionally neglect people in our immediate family. Many families created new routines to make "quality" time out of "quarantine" time. In a post–COVID-19 era that still calls for vigilance to remain protected from acquiring variants of the virus, keep quality time with family and friends a focus.

- Look for ways to practice gratitude and create opportunities for others to be grateful. Begin by reflecting upon people, experiences, and acts of consideration or kindness that you appreciate. Take time to share your appreciation by verbally telling someone the reason why who they are, how they *be*, or what they do makes a positive impact on your life, or write them a note to let them know of your gratitude. By doing so, you will create an opportunity for others to experience joy, love, kindness, or gratitude too.

BE ACCOUNTABLE AND EQUITABLE
(FOCUS: RESPONSIBLE DECISION-MAKING)

- Consistently practice physical distancing if designated as a required protocol by federal, state, or district standards. Remember, you are model for others—your children or nieces and nephews, your parents or grandparents, and your students. When we put into effect practices that protect others, we are modeling responsible decision-making. Wearing a mask in public is a good example. Many of us may feel awkward or express concern about how we look in a mask, but we still make a choice to wear it. Likewise, it is tempting to gather with friends who we love and care about, especially if we think they have been practicing appropriate physical distancing. Yet as responsible role-models, we must be patient and wait until the restrictions are lifted before we act in a way that could jeopardize the health of another.

- Be reliable. If you say you are going to do something, be sure to follow through. In times of adversity or uncertainty, people crave consistency. If for some reason you cannot keep your commitment, rather than making excuses be honest. Sincerely apologize and make a plan to make it right.

- Educators naturally have servants' hearts. This is an ideal time to help those in need. There are so many in our world today who are in need. Consider your strength and talents and determine at least one way in which you can help another human being. It may take time, talent, or financial resources—you choose. Now is the time to step into service.

- Take time to examine your implicit and explicit biases. Learn what it means to be culturally aware and responsive. Determine one way in which you can actively stand up against injustice or racism. Your approach does not need to be loud or public, but it does need to be informed, intentional, and authentic.

- Own your stuff. Any time we encounter the unknown, it is possible to step out in a way that offends or hurts another. When you are wrong, admit it. Forgive yourself and ask those negatively impacted to forgive you. We cannot learn, grow, or be forgiven if we don't first acknowledge when we mess up. Therefore, be willing to look at yourself and your part in any given situation.

- Ask for help. This is a tough time in our lives for so many reasons. So many people have lost so much. Most of us have lost our normal routines and activities. Some have lost support systems and stability that they had come to rely on. Many have lost jobs or savings. Others have experienced the ultimate loss of family or friends to this life-taking virus. It is devastating and traumatic. If you are feeling alone, anxious, depressed, or hopeless, it is courageous and responsible to ask for help. If you are not comfortable reaching out to a family member or friend you trust, there are resources available at www.samhsa.gov/find-help/disaster-distress-helpline.

I hope you found the Guidance for *Being* During Distance or Hybrid Education helpful. I also hope that as educators, and as humans, we have learned from what the pandemic *and* the social and racial reckoning that followed have taught us about ourselves and others. Finally, I hope that you have been empowered by the Framework for Social Emotional Well-Being and that you find in it a tool that enables you to reflect, recognize your strengths, and cultivate your social, emotional, mental, physical, and spiritual health.

Finally, although *Social Emotional Well-Being for Educators* is written for educators to address our social emotional well-being, one of the benefits of focusing first on ourselves is that we are better able to model and teach social emotional learning (SEL) skills to our students. In the following text, I have included a few general strategies for transferring our social emotional well-being lessons to our students through the lens of SEL.

Social Emotional Well-Being: Strategies for Students

....

SELF-AWARENESS

- Teach students to **be reflective.**
  - ○ Model being reflective in words and actions.
  - ○ Provide opportunities for students to practice reflection through writing responses or small-group discussion to specific prompts.
- Teach students to **put words to feelings**.
- Teach students to **name and notice** . . .
  - ○ Their emotions and the feelings that result from them.
  - ○ How those feelings manifest in their bodies.
  - ○ The difference they feel inside when they take a deep intentional breath.
- Use **affective questions** to help students to identify feelings or impact related to themselves and others, such as these:
  - ○ What happened?
  - ○ How might that impact you?
  - ○ How might that impact others?
  - ○ What do you think needs to happen now?
- Use **affective statements** to encourage and support students and to clearly communicate your needs.
  - ○ I appreciate the way you . . .
  - ○ I can see that you are using your (strength trait).
  - ○ I am frustrated when . . .
  - ○ I need to take a deep breath when . . .
- Teach students to use **affective language** to communicate their needs.
  - ○ I feel . . .
  - ○ When . . .
  - ○ Because . . .
  - ○ I need . . .
- Provide students with an emotional rating scale or use the Conscious Connection Chart to **identify emotions and feelings** in a way that is appropriate to their age, culture, and needs.
  - ○ Ensure privacy when checking in.
- **Identify** student **strengths** and express belief in those strengths by **telling students why you believe in them**.
- Help students develop self-efficacy.
  - ○ Provide opportunities for students to solution-seek and develop "**stick-to-it-iveness**."
  - ○ Reflect on negative feelings and acknowledge and explore failure as an opportunity for growth.

SELF-MANAGEMENT

- Teach students to **be intentional** in thoughts, words, and deeds.
  - Encourage them to think about the words they choose.
  - Provide opportunities for them to demonstrate kindness and gratitude.
  - Set expectations for students to use one another's names.
- Teach students to **notice feelings** and physical manifestations of feelings.
  - Teach a specific breathing strategy and ask students to notice the difference in their bodies before intentional breathing and then again after.
- Teach students to "think" in alignment with belief system.
  - Acknowledge the differences of belief systems based on family values, customs, or experiences, and encourage students to discuss with their families.
  - Remember to reflect on thought patterns following a negative outcome.
- Teach students the **power of** *choice*.
  - Identify opportunities to practice self-discipline.
  - Take it slow—incrementally—in order to promote success.
- Help students to **identify** that which is within their **realm of control**.
- Help students to allow feelings, including **failure**, to serve as a **self-motivator**.
- Introduce brain research regarding **positivity and self-confidence**.
- Teach **stress management** techniques, including breathing and/or meditation.
- Create opportunities for **movement**, including these:
  - Brain breaks
  - Flexible seating
  - Small-group discussions and activities
- Create and teach students to use a **Peace Place or Quiet Space** to center, reset, or focus.
  - Use a sand timer as a tool for students to monitor time and set expectations for self.
- Facilitate **restorative** practices for conflict resolution.
  - Use **"Tell me more . . ."** to help students identify what happened in a given situation, as well as the impact that their part in the situation may have had on others.
- Provide opportunities for students to **set and achieve goals**.

SOCIAL AWARENESS

- Define empathy and provide opportunities for students to **be empathetic.**
  - Use academics to teach empathy.
  - Facilitate small-group or whole-class activities to help students *feel* or experience the perspectives or life situations of others.
  - Create opportunities to **demonstrate acts of kindness** or to **serve others** within or outside of school community.
- Teach students to **see** one another for who they are **on the inside.**
  - Acknowledge similarities between people.
  - Acknowledge and provide opportunities to demonstrate **strength in diversity** or differences.
  - Provide opportunities for students to share strengths, interests, and talents.
  - Facilitate or train educators in providing **proactive relational restorative practices.**
- Meet **each student** where he/she/they are.
  - **Validate** strengths.
  - Identify and **remove** any potential **barriers** to learning.
  - **Differentiate** instruction to meet the academic, social, emotional, and behavior needs to each student.
- Teach the power of **perspective-taking** by modeling these steps:
  - **Seek to understand.**
  - Acknowledge others' feelings.
  - Acknowledge lessons learned from another.
- Provide opportunities for students to **share** their family **customs and traditions:**
  - Language
  - Music
  - Food
  - Other
- Define and discuss implicit or unintentional bias and provide encouragement for students to **practice humility** regarding another's culture, customs, or ways of being.
- Allow students to anonymously ask questions regarding race, ethnicity, and gender identity.
  - Review questions and create opportunities for discussion. Invite an administrator, school counselor or school social worker to join the discussion to provide expertise or support.
- **Encourage curiosity** and set expectations for respectful discussions, honoring opportunities for students to ask questions and share perspectives without judgment or criticism.

RELATIONSHIP SKILLS

- Establish a **daily routine**.
  - Greet each student by name.
  - Create a unique greeting for each student (contact or noncontact, as appropriate).
- Teach and practice ways to **be connected**.
  - *Stop* long enough to . . .
    - *Look* a student in the eye (if/when appropriate).
    - *Ask* "How are you?" or any other question.
    - *Listen* to the answer.
  - *Smile* authentically so that joy from your heart shines through your eyes.
  - *Connect* emotionally, socially, and kinesthetically (when appropriate and safe).
  - *Believe* intentionally in students' ability to achieve and in your own ability to make an impact on their learning.
- Be **intentional** while connecting with students.
  - Build trust.
  - Listen to them.
  - Validate them.
  - Allow opportunities for students to work together to find solutions.
  - Demonstrate positive regard.
- Facilitate opportunities for students to **build trust** with one another.
  - Create small-group or whole-class trust-building activities.
- Be aware of your **body language**.
  - An open stance, with hands at sides, palms open, and one foot slightly back is less threatening when a student feels frustrated or anxious.
  - When we cross our arms, roll our eyes, or turn away from students, our actions may indicate lack of caring or interest.
- Allow for small-group discussions and **collaboration** within each lesson.
- Teach and facilitate proactive practices to restore relationships.
  - Provide low-risk opportunities for students to share feelings, thoughts, or experiences.
  - Set expectations for **active listening** and honor the right to pass.
- Teach students **effective refusal skills**:
  - How to stand up for themselves and others in a respectful, assertive way.
  - How to say no by providing an authentic long-term reason, options to redirect, and ways to walk away if necessary.

RESPONSIBLE DECISION-MAKING

- Define and discuss what it means to **be accountable.**

- Teach the **power of choice** and provide opportunities for students to make choices.
  - Delineate the difference between mistake and choice, acknowledging the use of the word "mistake" can enable people to make excuses for their actions.
  - Engage students in the practice of autonomy.

- Teach the **ripple effect** and provide examples of the positive and negative impact of our choices.
  - Create reflection and discussion opportunities.

- Provide opportunities for students to practice being **reliable**.
  - Assign classroom tasks.
  - Emphasize the relationship between follow-through and being trustworthy.

- Teach and facilitate a decision-making process.

- Teach and facilitate an **accountability process** and set expectations for classroom or schoolwide investment.
  - Own a poor choice or part in what happened to negatively impact another.
  - Seek sincere forgiveness.
  - Make it right.
  - Create action plan to change behavior.

- Set and articulate **high expectations** for ALL students, and teach what it means to **be equitable.**

- Support use of check-in/check-out forms for students who benefit from **guided opportunity** to practice responsible decision-making.

- Teach and support **responsible use** of technology.

Finally, as our journey through *Social Emotional Well-Being for Educators* draws to a close, I want to thank you for who you are and all you do in this moment as teachers, administrators, school counselors and social workers, bus drivers, paraprofessionals, and office staff, as well as any other role you serve to support our school communities. You are someone wonderful! Remember that one of the most important ways to ignite hope for our students and their families today is to, first and foremost, take time to ignite hope in our own lives and that of our own families. Here are a few reminders:

- Take time to breathe. Be still for at least a few minutes each morning to remind yourself that this is a marathon, not a sprint, and it is okay to slow down.

- Give yourself grace. You don't have to be perfect.

- Recognize your strengths. You possess a character strength that will make a positive difference in this moment and each moment that follows.

- Practice gratitude. Each day, recognize a person, place, or experience for which you are grateful, and bless another with an act of kindness to give that person a reason to be grateful as well.

- Experience joy. Focus on doing at least one thing every day to make your heart smile. Be encouraged to remember that joy can always be found in the little things, like sharing a smile, interacting with a toddler, appreciating nature, or counting your blessings.

- And remember that only *you* have the capacity to reflect on your own well-being and pursue opportunities to grow. Take time to revisit the Social Emotional Well-Being Check-In throughout the year in order to reflect, refine, and grow. Please visit **resources.corwin.com/ SocialEmotionalWellBeingforEducators** to download a blank template.

Thank you for joining me on this journey! Please know that all these reminders, as well as the content and activities we explored as we traversed through these pages, will surely nourish our social emotional well-being and bring peace and hope to our hearts, minds, bodies, and souls, ultimately helping us to feel refreshed and renewed, which is essential because we are educators and we are Ignitors of Hope! This is our call to *Be!*

A NEW LESSON PLAN

It is July 2021—summertime. So many times over the last few months I have heard people refer to getting back to "normal." Though our world is still reeling from the COVID-19 pandemic, currently impacted most by the Delta variant, vaccinations are now available and seem to be effective against the virus. People are socializing again, and many schools are returning to in-person learning. Yet I wonder, do we truly want to return to normal?

When I think back to prepandemic, educators were stuck in a "feeling-overwhelmed, too-much-on-my-plate, I-can't-breathe" mentality. We talked the equity talk well. But we often neglected to actually walk it as we avoided conversations and data underscoring disproportionalities related to race, ethnicity, ability, gender, and socioeconomic status. For so many educators, "normal" completely neglected their social emotional well-being.

I think about the administrative cohort with whom I have been meeting virtually for over a year. We will actually be gathering in-person for the first time at the beginning of next month. We chose the beginning of August in the hope that we will have had a chance to relax over the summer, at least for a week or two, and that we will feel refreshed and renewed. It is not an easy task based on the continued challenges that lie ahead, yet together, we have reassessed, reflected, and refined. We have encouraged one another for over a year, and these educational leaders have focused on the importance of nurturing their own social emotional well-being so that they will be better prepared to model, encourage, and teach their staff and students to do the same.

As I prepare for our in-person meeting, I wonder if perhaps this is the lesson plan that is essential for all. What if we eradicate what was normal and establish a new norm? One in which we embrace this lesson called life. One in which we nourish our social emotional well-being by being reflective, intentional, empathetic, connected, accountable, and equitable. What if within our new norm we authentically model this way of being for our students? Maybe even for their families—and our own?

I am eager to meet with my administrative cohort and plan with them a new lesson that nurtures our social emotional well-being and cultivates hope.

But first, I put this way of being into practice as I grab my cup of coffee, smile at my husband, and pause for a moment to breathe, reflect, and connect.

Michelle L. Trujillo

MEET THE AUTHOR AND THE THOUGHT PARTNERS

About the Author

Michelle L. Trujillo is passionate about igniting hope in schools and the workplace! She is known to make a tangible, sustainable, and positive difference through her books, speaking engagements, and interactive workshops. Michelle shares enthusiasm, experience, and applicable takeaways with her audience. Her sincerity, enthusiasm, and expertise are contagious and substantial. Named Nevada's 2016 Innovative Educator of the Year, Michelle has appeared on television (including *Oprah*) and radio stations across the nation as a guest expert. A lifelong educator, Michelle is the author of *Start With the Heart: Igniting Hope in Schools Through Social and Emotional Learning*; *Thriving Through Adversity: Powerful Strategies for Educators to Ignite Hope, Inspire Students, and Transform Schools*; *Why Can't We Talk: What Teens Would Share if Parents Would Listen*; and *Chicken Soup for the Soul Presents Teens Talkin' Faith*. Michelle is the co-founder of the Center for Learning and Well-Being, and she invites you to visit www.center forlearningandwellbeing.com for resources and professional learning opportunities.

Meet the Thought Partners

Kori Hamilton Biagas is an educator, connector, truth seeker, master facilitator, and the founder of Just Educators. Kori founded Just Educators out of a deep passion to address social and educational inequity and injustice. Meeting people where they are in an authentic and respectful manner is core to her approach and is essential to changing hearts and minds. She uses her experiences to build connections and capacity in communities to dismantle systems and transform beliefs where racial inequity and social injustice exist. Find more information at www.justeducators.com.

Lori Nathanson, PhD, is a strategy/research/training consultant dedicated to equity and excellence in education. As a researcher with expertise in emotional intelligence (EQ), she values both evidence and emotions. At Duke University and the University of Virginia, Lori earned degrees and gained a wealth of experience in the fields of EQ and social and emotional learning (SEL). She used this knowledge as both a researcher and director of programs at NYU and Yale. She founded Lori Nathanson Consulting with the goal of sharing evidence-based practices that help adults and children alike to strengthen their EQ, be their best selves, and build more equitable learning and work environments. Learn more and reach out to Lori at www.lorinathanson.com.

Co-founder of the Center for Learning and Well-Being, **Taryn Waters** is passionate about helping educators do their jobs better and has a proven track record of creating sustained impact and value for mission-driven organizations. Over the course of her career, Taryn has developed comprehensive education strategies and solutions for hundreds of PreK–12 school systems and dozens of universities, including the development and launch of the largest evidence-based database in the world on what works best to improve teaching and learning.

ACKNOWLEDGMENTS

When I was a principal, we chose a theme on which to focus throughout every school year. One of my favorites was "Live Gratitude!" When gratitude is in our hearts and we speak it out, it acknowledges others. When we live it out in our attitudes and actions, it honors them! I hope to do both with the gratitude that I feel for those who helped this book to become a reality:

- Mike Soules and Jessica Allan, president of Corwin and most excellent editor—Thank you and your amazing team at Corwin for believing in this manuscript and for publishing it with a swift and sincere determination to get it into the hands of educators! And to Amy Schroller and Amy Hanquist Harris—I appreciate your diligence and effort through the editing process. I am grateful for both of you!

- Taryn Waters—My heart is full of gratitude for your vision, business aptitude, and willingness to step with me into the adventure that has become the Center for Learning and Well-Being!

- Kori Hamilton Biagas and Lori Nathanson—You authentically and consistently walk the walk of equity. I am grateful for both of you and your knowledge, perspective, and collaboration in developing the Conscious Connection Chart and Challenge!

- Ashley Greenwald and Maurice Elias—Thank you for sharing your wisdom with me and our readers. You are both phenomenal human beings, and I appreciate you!

- The Pod—You know who you are! In the loneliest moments of the pandemic, we relied on each other for friendship, challenging conversation, and lots of laughter! Vocationally, we collaborate to enhance the social emotional well-being of students and educators. In all of you, I have found inspiration and purpose in this work!

- Sharalee Jorgensen, my aunt and GodMom—Thank you for joining me in yet another writing adventure! This manuscript contains a continuity and clarity that could not have been achieved without your insight as an educator and expertise as an editor!

- Gary, Judy, and Jaime Williams, my parents and my sister—With Kelly in our hearts, we are five. The lessons I have learned from each of you fill my heart with so much gratitude and love that words are just not enough. Thank you for your constant love and encouragement as I pursue each writing project and life endeavor. I love you all! And to Velma, my mother-in-law—The time we spent together during the pandemic was filled with love and laughter in addition to quality conversations that enriched specific ideas within this manuscript. Thank you!

- David Trujillo, my husband—You! I'm grateful for you. Within these pages, I referred to the way your insight brings balance to my *way of being.* I am grateful for that and for your steadfast love and consistent reminder that *it's about the journey!* I love you and our journey! And to Corey and Dani, our children—I am grateful to each of you for the joy you bring, the lessons you teach, and the laughter you share. I love you both and dedicate this book to you!

- And to God, from whom all lessons flow—As always, thank You.

REFERENCES

Aos, Steve, Roxanne Lieb, Jim Mayfield, Marna Miller, and Annie Pennucci. 2004. *Benefits and Costs of Prevention and Early Intervention Programs for Youth.* Olympia, WA: Washington State Institute for Public Policy.

Bandura, Albert. 1986. *Social Foundations of Thought and Action: A Social Cognitive Theory*, 21. Englewood Cliffs, NJ: Prenctice Hall.

Boss, Suzie. 2012. "PBL Teachers Need Time to Reflect, Too." *Edutopia.* George Lucas Educational Foundation, November 28. www.edutopia.org/blog/project-learning-teacher-reflection-suzie-boss.

CASEL. 2020 November. "What Is the CASEL Framework?" casel.org/what-is-sel/.

Coelho, Paulo, Alan Clarke, and James Noel Smith. 2014. *The Alchemist.* New York: Harper Luxe, an Imprint of HarperCollins Publishers.

Colonnello, Valentina, Nicola Petrocchi, Marina Farinelli, and Cristina Ottaviani. 2017. "Positive Social Interactions in a Lifespan Perspective With a Focus on Opioidergic and Oxytocinergic Systems: Implications for Neuroprotection." *Current Neuropharmacology* 15 (4): 543–61. doi:10.2174/1570159X14666160816120209.

Durlak, Joseph A., Roger P. Weissberg, Allison B. Dymnicki, Rebecca D. Taylor, and Kriston B. Schellinger. 2011. "The Impact of Enhancing Students' Social and Emotional Learning: A Meta-Analysis of School-Based Universal Interventions." *Child Development* 82 (1): 405–32.

Ferguson, Donna. 2019. "Record Levels of Stress 'Put Teachers at Breaking Point.'" *The Guardian*, Guardian News and Media, November 10. www.theguardian.com/education/2019/nov/10/stressed-teachers-at-breaking-point-says-report.

Greenwald, Ashley. 2021. Written Interview Response. By Michelle L. Trujillo. April 15.

Hamilton Biagas, Kori. 2021a. Written Interview Response. By Michelle L. Trujillo. July 15.

Hamilton Biagas, Kori. 2021b. Written response to interview questions. By Michelle L. Trujillo. March.

Hawkins, J. David, Rick Kosterman, Richard F. Catalano, Karl G. Hill, and Robert D. Abbott. 2005. "Promoting Positive Adult Functioning Through Social Development Intervention in Childhood: Long-Term Effects From the Seattle Social Development Project." *Archives of Pediatrics & Adolescent Medicine* 159 (1): 25–31.

Maxwell, John C. 2017. *Intentional Living: Choosing a Life That Matters*. New York: Center Street.

Nathanson, Lori. 2021. Interview. By Michelle L. Trujillo. July 13.

National Museum of African American History and Culture. 2021. "National Museum of African American History and Culture Releases 'Talking About Race' Web Portal." https://nmaahc.si .edu/about/news/national-museum-african-american-history-and-culture-releases-talking-about-race-web.

Perda, David. 2013. *Transitions Into and Out of Teaching: A Longitudinal Analysis of Early Career Teacher Turnover*. Philadelphia: University of Pennsylvania Press.

Simmons, Dena. 2019. "Why We Can't Afford Whitewashed Social-Emotional Learning." *ASCD*, April 1. https://www .ascd.org/el/articles/why-we-cant-afford-whitewashed-social-emotional-learning.

Summitt, Pat, and Sally Jenkins. 1999. *Reach for the Summit: The Definite Dozen System for Succeeding at Whatever You Do*, 39. New York: Broadway Books.

Thoreau, Henry David. 1954. *Walden, or, Life in the Woods*, 13. New York: New American Library. Original work published 1919.

Walker, Tim. 2019. "'I Didn't Know It Had a Name': Secondary Traumatic Stress and Educators." *NEA Today*, December 18. neatoday.org/2019/10/18/secondary-traumatic-stress/.

A SAGE Publishing Company

CORWIN HAS ONE MISSION: to enhance education through intentional professional learning.

We build long-term relationships with our authors, educators, clients, and associations who partner with us to develop and continuously improve the best evidence-based practices that establish and support lifelong learning.

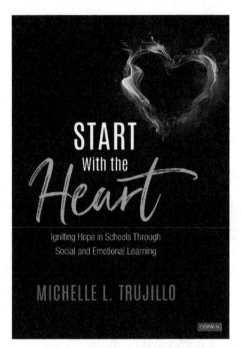

TMN21C22